COIN COLLECTING
FOR
BEGINNERS

Burton Hobson & Fred Reinfeld

W Published by
Melvin Powers
WILSHIRE BOOK COMPANY
12015 Sherman Road
No. Hollywood, California 91605
Telephone: (213) 875-1711

ACKNOWLEDGMENTS

The authors wish to thank the many collectors and dealers whose thoughts and suggestions have been incorporated in this project.

In compiling the values of coins for this volume, careful attention has been devoted to prices quoted in recent dealer advertisements and prices realized lists of auction sales, as well as the recognized published authorities.

The enlarged condition photographs were made by the American Numismatic Society.

Printed by
HAL LEIGHTON PRINTING COMPANY
P.O. Box 3952
North Hollywood, California 91605
Telephone: (213) 983-1105

Manufactured in the United States of America
Library of Congress Catalog Card. No. : 63–19156

ISBN 0-87980-022-4

CONTENTS

THE FUGIO CENT

The first coins struck by authority of the U.S. government were the "Fugio" cents of 1787. The motto meaning "time flies therefore tend to your business," is usually credited to Benjamin Franklin.

1. COINS AND THEIR VALUE

Collecting rare coins has been a pastime of the well-to-do since the days of the ancient Greeks and Romans. During the past several years, however, this interest has spread throughout the country until today we find housewives, newsboys, professional people, students, grandparents, white-collar and blue-collar workers building coin collections and all with a personal interest in coin valuations.

The popularity of coin collecting continues to grow. The Director of the Mint estimates there are now up to as many as 8,000,000 collectors—so many that the mint has been hard pressed to produce enough coins to satisfy all the demands.

Coins are fascinating in themselves, just for the history they represent. Their most intriguing feature, though, has been their spectacular rise in value over the past few years. This manual contains an up-to-date catalogue of coin prices for all the popularly collected series of U.S. coins. Here is the information you need to understand coin values and to take advantage of the coin market as a collector or investor.

The value of a given coin is a complex thing. The number of pieces struck during the year of issue naturally has much to do with it. As you would expect, an 1877 Indian Head cent with a mintage of fewer than one million pieces is worth about ten times as much as the older 1867 of which nearly ten million were made, and approximately 100 times as much as the 1887 with a coinage of 45 million pieces.

Closely related to the scarcity factor in the valuation of U.S. coins are mint marks. The mint marks are small letters indicating that a coin was struck at a branch mint rather than at Philadelphia. Many U.S. coins have been issued in a single year by two, three, four or, in a few instances, five different mints. In most of these cases, there is a considerable difference in the quantities struck at the various mints. Look at the 1950 nickels. The Denver mint coin is worth about five times as much as the Philadelphia nickel of the same date.

An older coin that collectors like to quote as an example of the importance of mint marks is the 1914 cent. A little "D" below the date of this coin makes it at least fifty times as valuable as the plain 1914 Philadelphia cent. The "S" mint coin of 1914 is worth about five times as much as the Philadelphia. Now can you see why it is essential to recognize mint marks and their significance in coin evaluation?

Another key element is the physical state of a coin—its condition. Coins in new, uncirculated condition—just as they left the mint— are obviously more attractive than worn or battered coins. They are so much more desirable, in fact, that coins in choice condition command substantial premiums over coins in average condition. A coin in brilliant, uncirculated condition can easily be worth ten times as much as the identical coin in used condition. On the other hand, mutilation or damage to a coin detracts from its value. Unless it is a rare date, a coin in poor condition is worth little or nothing to a collector.

A less tangible factor in coin values is demand—the degree of popularity with collectors of a coin or series of coins. The recorded mintage for the 1856 half cent is only 40,430 pieces; for the 1931-D cent it is 4,480,000. Yet the 75-year-newer Lincoln cent with a mintage more than 100 times as great is worth just as much as the half cent, simply because there is far greater interest in and demand for the Lincoln cent series. Knowing which coins are popular, being able to predict *which coins are likely to grow in demand*, is the key to successful coin investment.

The catalogue section lists the numismatic value of all the popularly-collected U.S. coins by date, mint mark and condition and shows the quantity minted for each coin. The sections following explain in greater detail the importance of supply and demand, condition and mint marks in arriving at coin values.

2. CATALOG OF U. S. COINS

The following tables give a comprehensive listing of all the regular issues of the United States Mint. You will note that the values depend on various types of condition, as described on pages 71-81.

The column on the extreme left of the tables gives the quantity of coins issued in a given year. Sometimes a total figure includes several varieties lumped together. In other cases the Mint reports have broken down the quantities that apply to each variety in a given year.

Wherever it seemed essential, individual varieties issued in the same year have been listed separately and carefully described in order to distinguish them from other varieties issued in the same year.

Note also that mint marks (described on pages 58-70) play an important part in determining valuation. In most cases—but not all—the *quantity* issued by each Mint will give you the clue to the *variations in value* between the coins of the different Mints.

Small Cents

FLYING EAGLE CENTS

Quantity	Year	Good	Very Good	Fine	Very Fine	Ext. Fine	Unc.
* 1,000	1856 rare	$750.00	$850.00	$1200.00	$1300.00	$1600.00	$2500.00
17,450,000	1857	10.00	12.50	15.00	25.00	60.00	500.00
24,600,000 {	1858 large letters	10.00	12.50	15.00	25.00	60.00	500.00
	1858 small letters	10.00	12.50	15.00	25.00	70.00	500.00

Indian Head Cent

UNCIRCULATED

All details of the design are extremely clear. Note especially the fine detail in the feathers and the hair, the beads in the necklace, the diamonds on the ribbon, the fullness of the facial features and the clarity of LIBERTY on the headband.

VERY FINE

Portions of the leaves in the shield show smooth spots. The vertical lines of the shield are clear but the horizontal lines are no longer sharp.

VERY GOOD

The outline of the head, letters and date are clear but much worn. LIBERTY is gone, no beads show and no detail is visible in the feathers. The top outine of the headband still shows.

INDIAN HEAD CENTS
(White Copper-Nickel, thick)

Quantity	Year	Good	Very Good	Fine	Very Fine	Ext. Fine	Unc.
36,400,000	1859	$4.00	$6.50	$10.00	$20.00	$55.00	$325.00

Quantity	Year	Good	Very Good	Fine	Very Fine	Ext. Fine	Unc.
20,566,000	1860	3.50	5.00	8.00	12.50	25.00	100.00
10,100,000	1861	7.50	12.50	17.50	25.00	35.00	135.00
28,075,000	1862	3.25	5.00	6.50	9.00	17.50	85.00
49,840,000	1863	3.00	4.00	5.50	9.00	16.50	85.00
13,740,000	1864	5.00	7.50	12.50	20.00	30.00	125.00

(Bronze)

Quantity	Year	Good	Very Good	Fine	Very Fine	Ext. Fine	Unc.
39,233,714	1864	$2.75	$4.50	$8.00	$16.50	27.50	$75.00
	1864 L on ribbon rare	12.50	25.00	45.00	65.00	90.00	275.00
35,429,286	1865	2.50	3.50	7.50	15.00	25.00	65.00
9,826,500	1866	15.00	20.00	30.00	45.00	70.00	140.00
9,821,000	1867	15.00	20.00	30.00	45.00	70.00	140.00
10,266,500	1868	15.00	20.00	30.00	45.00	70.00	140.00
	1869 over 68	60.00	100.00	200.00	300.00	425.00	850.00
6,420,000	1869	20.00	35.00	60.00	85.00	125.00	300.00
5,275,000	1870	17.50	30.00	50.00	65.00	90.00	200.00
3,929,500	1871	22.50	35.00	65.00	80.00	115.00	225.00
4,042,000	1872	25.00	40.00	70.00	95.00	135.00	275.00
11,676,500	1873	5.00	8.50	16.50	25.00	50.00	85.00
14,187,500	1874	5.00	8.50	16.50	25.00	50.00	85.00
13,528,000	1875	5.00	8.50	16.50	25.00	50.00	85.00
7,944,000	1876	8.50	12.00	25.00	32.50	50.00	110.00
852,500	1877	125.00	175.00	275.00	375.00	550.00	1000.00
5,799,955	1878	8.00	12.50	30.00	45.00	60.00	110.00
16,231,200	1879	2.00	3.50	7.50	15.00	20.00	50.00
38,964,955	1880	1.25	2.00	3.25	5.25	10.00	37.50
39,211,575	1881	1.25	2.00	3.25	5.25	10.00	37.50
38,581,100	1882	1.25	2.00	3.25	5.25	10.00	37.50
45,598,109	1883	1.25	2.00	3.25	5.25	10.00	37.50

INDIAN HEAD CENTS (continued)

Quantity	Year	Good	Very Good	Fine	Very Fine	Ext. Fine	Unc.
23,261,742	1884	1.75	3.00	6.00	10.00	15.00	50.00
11,765,384	1885	3.25	6.00	9.00	15.00	25.00	60.00
17,654,290	1886	2.00	3.00	7.50	9.00	18.50	55.00
45,226,483	1887	1.00	1.25	2.00	3.50	10.00	40.00
37,494,414	1888	1.00	1.25	2.00	3.50	10.00	40.00
48,869,361	1889	1.00	1.25	2.00	3.50	10.00	40.00
57,182,854	1890	1.00	1.25	2.00	3.50	10.00	40.00
47,072,350	1891	1.00	1.25	2.00	3.50	10.00	40.00
37,649,832	1892	1.00	1.25	2.00	3.50	10.00	40.00
46,642,195	1893	1.00	1.25	2.00	3.50	10.00	40.00
16,752,132	1894	1.65	5.00	7.00	11.00	16.50	50.00
38,343,636	1895	.75	1.00	1.50	3.00	8.00	35.00
39,057,293	1896	.75	1.00	1.50	3.00	8.00	35.00
50,466,330	1897	.75	1.00	1.50	3.00	8.00	35.00
49,823,079	1898	.75	1.00	1.50	3.00	8.00	35.00
53,600,031	1899	.75	1.00	1.50	3.00	8.00	35.00
66,833,764	1900	.70	.85	1.35	2.50	7.50	35.00
79,611,143	1901	.70	.85	1.35	2.50	7.50	32.50
87,376,722	1902	.70	.85	1.35	2.50	7.50	32.50
85,094,493	1903	.70	.85	1.35	2.50	7.50	32.50
61,328,015	1904	.70	.85	1.35	2.50	7.50	32.50
80,719,163	1905	.70	.85	1.35	2.50	7.50	32.50
96,022,255	1906	.70	.85	1.35	2.50	7.50	32.50
108,138,618	1907	.70	.85	1.35	2.50	7.50	32.50
32,327,987	1908	.75	.90	1.50	3.00	7.50	37.50
1,115,000	1908 S	18.00	20.00	25.00	30.00	45.00	135.00
14,370,645	1909	1.10	1.50	1.75	3.50	8.00	40.00
309,000	1909 S	70.00	80.00	100.00	110.00	150.00	300.00

The "S" mint mark on the 1908 and 1909 issues is at the bottom of the reverse under the wreath.

HOW TO RECOGNIZE VARIETIES

The "A" and "M" of "AMERICA" are joined on the large letter 1858 Flying Eagle cent; they are detached on the small letter variety.

On the 1864-L bronze Indian Head cent, the designer's initial appears on the bonnet ribbon. Hold the coin so the Indian faces you and tip the coin slightly to highlight the letter.

The 1869/68 overdate Indian Head cent shows the loop of another numeral between the knob and circle of the "9."

Lincoln Head Cent

UNCIRCULATED

The details of Lincoln's hair, beard and features are sharp and clear. The lines of his coat, shirt and tie are distinct.

EXTREMELY FINE

The lines of the wheat stalk are clear and distinct. There is slight wear on the inside row of grains.

VERY FINE

Definite wear shows in the hair around the ear. There is a smooth spot at the top of the ear.

Lincoln Head Cent

FINE

The parallel lines of the stalk have smooth areas, particularly near the top of the left stalk. Each grain is visible but no longer sharply defined.

VERY GOOD

All fine detail is gone from the hair and beard. Only a rough outline of the ear is visible. The left end of the bowtie is only vague.

GOOD

The lines of the wheat stalks are worn smooth. Only the vaguest outline of the grains can be seen.

LINCOLN HEAD CENTS

The mint mark is on the obverse under the date.

Quantity	Year	Good	Very Good	Fine	Very Fine	Ext. Fine	Unc.
27,995,000	1909 VDB	$1.75	$2.00	$2.25	$2.50	$3.50	$13.50
484,000	1909 S VDB	150.00	165.00	185.00	210.00	235.00	350.00
72,702,618	1909 plain	.40	.45	.50	.80	1.50	10.00
1,825,000	1909 S plain	27.50	30.00	32.50	40.00	50.00	85.00
146,801,218	1910	.15	.30	.50	.80	1.75	10.00
6,045,000	1910 S	6.00	6.50	7.50	8.50	11.50	50.00
101,177,787	1911	.15	.30	.65	1.25	4.00	12.50
4,026,000	1911 S	10.00	11.00	12.50	15.00	20.00	65.00
12,672,000	1911 D	2.50	3.50	5.00	8.50	15.00	60.00
68,153,060	1912	.20	.40	1.65	3.75	6.00	.25.00
4,431,000	1912 S	9.00	10.00	12.50	16.00	22.50	65.00
10,411,000	1912 D	2.50	3.50	5.00	10.00	20.00	60.00
76,532,352	1913	.20	.35	1.25	3.75	6.50	20.00
6,101,000	1913 S	5.00	5.50	6.50	8.00	15.00	55.00
15,804,000	1913 D	1.25	1.75	3.00	6.75	15.00	55.00
75,238,432	1914	.20	.35	2.00	4.00	7.50	32.50
4,137,000	1914 S	6.75	7.50	8.50	11.00	20.00	75.00
1,193,000	1914 D	60.00	65.00	70.00	100.00	200.00	800.00
29,092,120	1915	.60	1.25	4.50	9.00	20.00	70.00
4,833,000	1915 S	5.50	6.00	7.00	10.00	15.00	60.00
22,050,000	1915 D	.75	1.00	1.25.	5.00	9.50	30.00
131,833,677	1916	.15	.20	.35	.75	3.00	10.00
22,510,000	1916 S	.50	.80	1.25	2.50	6.00	35.00
35,956,000	1916 D	.20	.35	1.00	2.75	6.50	25.00
196,429,785	1917	.15	.20	.35	.75	2.00	10.00
32,620,000	1917 S	.20	.40	.65	2.50	5.25	35.00
55,120,000	1917 D	.20	.30	.65	2.75	6.50	35.00
288,104,634	1918	.15	.20	.35	.75	4.00	12.00
34,680,000	1918 S	.20	.30	.50	2.25	4.50	35.00
47,830,000	1918 D	.20	.30	.60	2.25	5.00	35.00
392,021,000	1919	.15	.20	.30	.60	1.75	9.00
139,760,000	1919 S	.20	.30	.40	1.25	2.50	18.00
57,154,000	1919 D	.20	.30	.65	2.75	5.00	22.50
310,165,000	1920	.15	.20	.30	.65	1.75	9.00
46,220,000	1920 S	.15	.20	.50	1.50	4.00	32.50
49,280,000	1920 D	.15	.20	.55	1.50	4.00	35.00
39,157,000	1921	.20	.25	.50	1.00	4.50	30.00
15.274.000	1921 S	.60	.75	1.00	2.50	9.00	185.00
	1922	100.00	$110.00	135.00	175.00	300.00	1850.00
7,160,000	1922 D	6.00	6.50	7.50	9.00	12.50	55.00
74,723,000	1923	.15	.20	.35	.60	1.75	10.00
8,700,000	1923 S	1.50	1.75	2.00	4.50	15.00	275.00
75,178,000	1924	.15	.20	.35	.60	3.25	22.50
11,696,000	1924 S	.50	.75	1.00	2.25	5.50	120.00
2,520,000	1924 D	8.00	9.00	10.00	13.50	28.00	275.00
139,949,000	1925	.15	.20	.35	.60	2.50	8.00
26,380,000	1925 S	.15	.25	.40	1.00	3.50	50.00
22,580,000	1925 D	.25	.35	.55	1.10	4.00	40.00

LINCOLN HEAD CENTS (continued)

Quantity	Year	Good	Very Good	Fine	Very Fine	Ext. Fine	Unc.
157,088,000	1926	.15	.20	.35	.60	2.50	9.00
4,550,000	1926 S	3.00	3.50	+.00	5.00	12.50	150.00
28,020,000	1926 D	.20	.30	.50	1.00	3.00	35.00
144,440,000	1927	.15	.20	.30	.90	2.50	9.00
14,276,000	1927 S	.30	.40	.75	1.75	4.00	50.00
27,170,000	1927 D	.20	.30	.50	.75	2.00	25.00
134,116,000	1928	.15	.20	.30	.40	2.50	9.00
17,266,000	1928 S	.25	.80	.35	.90	2.25	40.00
31,170,000	1928 D	.20	.25	.30	.60	1.50	20.00
185,262,000	1929	.15	.20	.30	.50	1.25	8.00
50,148,000	1929 S	.15	.20	.30	.50	1.25	10.00
41,730,000	1929 D	.15	.20	.30	.50	1.25	12.50
157,415,000	1930	.10	.15	.20	.35	1.00	8.00
24,286,000	1930 S	.10	.15	.20	.50	1.50	9.00
40,100,000	1930 D	.10	.15	.20	.45	1.00	10.00
19,396,000	1931	.20	.25	.30	.55	1.50	17.50
866,000	1931 S	25.00	27.50	30.00	32.50	35.00	60.00
4,480,000	1931 D	2.75	3.25	3.50	4.00	7.00	55.00
9,062,000	1932	1.00	1.25	1.50	2.00	2.75	17.50
10,500,000	1932 D	.65	.75	1.25	2.00	2.50	15.00
14,360,000	1933	.50	.60	.70	.90	2.00	17.50
6,200,000	1933 D	1.75	2.00	2.25	2.50	3.50	22.50

Quantity	Year	Unc.	Quantity	Year	Unc.
219,080,000	1934	$3.25	282,760,000	1944 S copper	$ .35
28,446,000	1934 D	20.00	430,587,000	1944 D copper	.30
245,388,000	1935	1.75	1,040,515,000	1945 copper	.30
38,702,000	1935 S	6.50	181,770,000	1945 S copper	.50
47,000,000	1935 D	2.50	226,268,000	1945 D copper	.60
309,637,569	1936	2.00	991,655,000	1946	.25
29,130,000	1936 S	2.00	198,100,000	1946 S	.50
40,620,000	1936 D	1.75	315,690,000	1946 D	.25
309,179,320	1937	1.75	190,555,000	1947	.70
34,500,000	1937 S	2.00	99,000,000	1947 S	.70
50,430,000	1937 D	2.00	194,750,000	1947 D	.35
156,696,734	1938	1.85	317,570,000	1948	.50
15,180,000	1938 S	4.00	81,735,000	1948 S	1.00
20,010,000	1938 D	3.00	172,637,500	1948 D	.30
316,479,520	1939	1.25	217,490,000	1949	.75
52,070,000	1939 S	1.75	64,290,000	1949 S	1.50
15,160,000	1939 D	5.00	154,370,500	1949 D	.60
586,825,872	1940	1.00	272,686,386	1950	.40
112,940,000	1940 S	.90	118,505,000	1950 S	.65
81,390,000	1940 D	1.00	334,950,000	1950 D	.30
887,039,100	1941	.75	294,633,500	1951	1.50
92,360,000	1941 S	4.00	100,890,000	1951 S	1.00
128,700,000	1941 D	3.00	625,355,000	1951 D	.20
657,828,600	1942	.50	186,856,980	1952	.60
85,590,000	1942 S	5.00	137,800,004	1952 S	.65
206,698,000	1942 D	.70	746,130,000	1952 D	.20
684,628,670	1943 zinc-steel	.60	256,883,800	1953	.20
191,550,000	1943 S zinc-steel	1.75	181,835,000	1953 S	.45
217,660,000	1943 D zinc-steel	.75	700,515,000	1953 D	.20
1,435,400,000	1944 copper	.35	71,873,350	1954	.50
282,760,000	1944 S copper	.30	563,257,500	1955 D	.15
430,587,000	1944 D copper	.30	420,926,081	1956	.15
1,040,515,000	1945 copper	.30	1,098,201,100	1956 D	.10
181,770,000	1945 S copper	.40	282,540,000	1957	.15
226,268,000	1945 D copper	.30	1,051,342,000	1957 D	.10
991,655,000	1946	.20	252,595,000	1958	.15
198,100,000	1946 S	.35	800,953,300	1958 D	.10

LINCOLN HEAD CENTS (continued)

Quantity	Year	Unc.
619,715,000	1959	.10
1,279,760,000	1959 D	.10
586,405,000	1960 Small date	5.00
	1960 Large date	.10
1,580,884,000	1960 D Small date	.35
	1960 D Large date	.10
756,373,244	1961	.10
1,753,266,700	1961 D	.10
609,263,019	1962	.10
1,793,148,400	1962 D	.10
757,185,645	1963	.10
1,774,020,400	1963 D	.10
2,648,575,000	1964	.10
3,799,071,500	1964 D	.10
1,494,884,900	1965	.10
2,185,886,200	1966	.10
3,048,667,100	1967	.10
1,707,880,970	1968	.10
2,886,269,600	1968 D	.10
258,270,001	1968 S	.10
1,136,910,000	1969	.10
4,002,832,200	1969 D	.10
544,375,000	1969 S	.10
1,898,315,000	1970	.10
2,891,438,900	1970 D	.10
693,192,814	1970 S	.10
	1971	.10
	1971 D	.10
	1971 S	.10

Quantity	Year	Unc.
	1972 Double strike	175.00
2,933,255,000	1972	.10
2,665,071,400	1972 D	.10
380,200,104	1972 S	.10
3,728,245,000	1973	.10
3,549,576,588	1973 D	.10
319,937,634	1973 S	.10
4,232,140,523	1974	.10
4,235,098,000	1974 D	.10
412,039,228	1974 S	.10
5,451,476,142	1975	
4,505,275,300	1975 D	.10
	1975 S (proof only)	
4,674,292,426	1976	.10
4,221,592,455	1976 D	.10
	1976 S (proof only)	
4,469,930,000	1977	.10
4,194,062,300	1977 D	.10
	1977 S (proof only)	
5,558,605,000	1978	.10
4,280,233,400	1978 D	.10
	1978 S (proof only)	
	1979	.10
	1979 D	.10
	1979 S (proof only)	

On 1960 large date cents, the top of the "9" extends above the "1," "6" has a long tail and the "0" is decidedly round. On the small date variety, the top of the "1" extends above the "9," "6" has a short tail and the "0" is oval shaped.

The 1955 "double die" variety shows a shadow impression of the date and legends on the obverse.

Nickel Five Cents

SHIELD NICKELS

1866 - 1867   1867 - 1883

Quantity	Year	Good to Very Good	Fine	Very Fine	Ext. Fine	Unc.
14,742,500	1866	$11.00	$17.00	$27.50	$85.00	$415.00
30,909,500 {	1867 with rays	13.50	25.00	35.00	90.00	425.00
	1867 without rays	8.00	12.50	17.50	35.00	175.00
28,817,000	1868	8.00	12.50	17.50	35.00	175.00
16,395,000	1869	8.00	12.50	17.50	35.00	175.00
4,806,000	1870	10.00	14.00	20.00	37.50	200.00
561,000	1871	35.00	45.00	55.00	85.00	325.00
6,036,000	1872	9.00	15.00	17.50	30.00	175.00
4,550,000	1873	9.50	12.50	20.00	35.00	175.00
3,538,000	1874	11.00	17.50	18.00	40.00	175.00
2,097,000	1875	12.50	22.50	27.50	50.00	250.00
2,530,000	1876	12.00	20.00	25.00	40.00	200.00
?500	1877 only proofs were struck					
2,350	1878 only proofs were struck					
29,100	1879	85.00	100.00	135.00	175.00	375.00
19,955	1880	100.00	135.00	150.00	200.00	400.00
72,375	1881	85.00	125.00	140.00	200.00	375.00
11,476,600	1882	9.00	12.50	20.00	30.00	175.00
1,456,919	1883	10.00	12.50	20.00	30.00	175.00

Liberty Head Nickel UNCIRCULATED

The design perfectly clear. Much fine detail is apparent in the hair, coronet and spray of leaves. The majority of the stars show points depending upon how sharply struck the coin is.

Liberty Head Nickel

VERY FINE

Design sharp but definite signs of wear begin to show. Smooth areas appear in the hair above the ear and in the chignon (bun) at back of the head. All letters in LIBERTY visible and strong except possibly the I which must at least show.

VERY GOOD

A much worn coin. All details of the hair are gone. The cheek and jawline are smooth. LIBERTY will not show more than parts of two or three letters.

GOOD

A really minimum condition, smooth coin. The date is readable but all fullness of the design is gone. The head shows up in outline only. Denticles at the edge of the coin are worn down.

1883   1883-1912

The variety without "CENTS" was issued first, but unscrupulous people goldplated them and passed them off as $5 gold pieces. To remedy the situation, the word "CENTS" was added to the later issues and continued to appear on subsequent dates

Quantity	Year	Good	Very Good	Fine	Very Fine	Ext. Fine	Unc.
5,479,519	1883 without "Cents"....	$2.25	$3.00	$3.50	$6.00	$9.00	$45.00
16,032,983	1883 with "Cents"....	6.50	8.50	17.50	25.00	37.50	140.00
11,273,942	1884	7.00	9.00	18.50	27.50	45.00	150.00
1,476,490	1885	115.00	150.00	200.00	240.00	275.00	425.00
3,330,290	1886	35.00	50.00	75.00	100.00	150.00	225.00
15,263,652	1887	3.50	5.00	12.50	20.00	35.00	135.00
10,720,483	1888	6.50	10.00	17.50	22.50	37.50	150.00
15,881,361	1889	3.50	5.00	12.50	20.00	35.00	135.00
16,259,272	1890	4.50	6.00	15.00	22.50	37.50	135.00
16,834,350	1891	3.50	5.00	12.50	20.00	35.00	135.00
11,699,642	1892	3.50	5.00	12.50	20.00	35.00	135.00
13,370,195	1893	3.50	5.00	12.50	20.00	35.00	150.00
5,413,132	1894	7.00	9.00	18.50	27.50	45.00	150.00
9,979,884	1895	2.50	5.00	12.50	17.50	30.00	150.00
8,842,920	1896	3.00	6.00	15.00	20.00	25.00	150.00
20,428,735	1897	1.00	2.00	4.00	7.00	22.50	125.00
12,532,087	1898	1.00	2.00	4.00	7.00	22.50	125.00
26,029,031	1899	.75	1.75	4.00	6.50	22.50	125.00
27,255,995	1900	.75	1.00	3.00	6.00	20.00	120.00
26,480,213	1901	.75	1.00	3.00	6.00	20.00	120.00
31,480,579	1902	.75	1.00	3.00	6.00	20.00	120.00
28,006,725	1903	.75	1.00	3.00	6.00	20.00	120.00
21,404,984	1904	.75	1.00	3.00	6.00	20.00	120.00
29,827,276	1905	.75	1.00	3.00	6.00	20.00	120.00
38,613,725	1906	.75	1.00	3.00	6.00	20.00	120.00
39,214,800	1907	.75	1.00	3.00	6.00	20.00	120.00
22,686,177	1908	.75	1.00	3.00	6.00	20.00	120.00
11,590,526	1909	.75	1.00	3.00	6.00	20.00	120.00
30,169,353	1910	.75	1.00	3.00	6.00	20.00	120.00
39,559,372	1911	.75	1.00	3.00	6.00	20.00	120.00
26,236,714	1912	.75	1.00	3.00	6.00	20.00	120.00
8,474,000	*1912 D	2.50	3.50	12.50	15.00	60.00	235.00
238,000	*1912 S	30.00	37.50	50.00	100.00	150.00	500.00
?	1913 (an outstanding rarity)						

* Mint mark to left of "CENTS" on reverse.

Liberty Head nickels were discontinued in 1912 but apparently 5 specimens dated 1913 were struck, thus creating one of the rarest U.S. coins. All 5 pieces are accounted for in leading collections.

Buffalo Nickel

UNCIRCULATED

The Indian's head does not have the same fine detail as designs of many other U.S. coins. Cheekbone is full, the date, feathers and braid are sharp.

UNCIRCULATED

The buffalo has a full, rounded horn and the tip of the tail shows distinctly. The blanket of hair on the shoulder is clearly defined.

EXTREMELY FINE

A slight spot of wear shows on the highest point, the ribbon on the braid of hair.

Buffalo Nickel

VERY FINE

The top of the horn is faded but distinct, much of the roundness is lost. The fine detail is gone from the shoulder hair.

FINE

The Indian's hair is considerably worn and the tops of the feathers are smooth. The date is faded but each digit is still legible.

VERY GOOD

Only the base of the horn remains. The shoulder and rear leg are worn smooth. The rim may be worn down into the edge of the lettering.

BUFFALO NICKELS

The mint marks are under "Five cents" on the reverse.

1913   1913-1938

Quantity	Year	Good	Very Good	Fine	Very Fine	Ext. Fine	Unc.
30,993,520	1913 Type 1—buffalo on mound	$2.50	$3.00	$4.00	$6.50	$10.00	$32.50
2,105,000	1913 S Type 1	6.00	8.50	10.00	15.00	18.00	65.00
5,337,000	1913 D Type 1	4.50	5.50	7.00	9.00	12.50	55.00
29,858,700	1913 Type 2—buffalo on line	2.50	3.00	3.50	4.50	7.00	30.00
1,209,000	1913 S Type 2	35.00	45.00	60.00	70.00	90.00	175.00
4,156,000	1913 D Type 2	25.00	30.00	35.00	45.00	55.00	115.00
20,665,738	1914	$3.00	4.00	5.00	6.50	10.00	40.00
3,470,000	1914 S	4.00	5.00	8.00	11.00	22.00	85.00
3,912,000	1914 D	17.50	20.00	30.00	40.00	60.00	160.00
20,987,270	1915	1.25	1.75	3.00	4.50	10.00	35.00
1,505,000	1915 S	7.00	10.00	20.00	40.00	50.00	165.00
7,569,500	1915 D	5.00	6.50	11.00	17.00	27.00	80.00
63,498,066	1916	.50	.85	1.50	2.50	6.00	30.00
11,860,000	1916 S	3.00	4.00	6.50	10.00	27.00	110.00
13,333,000	1916 D	3.50	4.50	6.50	9.00	22.00	100.00
51,424,029	1917	.60	.80	1.50	3.00	10.00	40.00
4,193,000	1917 S	2.50	5.50	9.00	22.50	45.00	175.00
9,910,800	1917 D	2.75	5.50	9.00	23.00	40.00	165.00
32,086,314	1918	.50	1.00	2.00	5.00	12.00	75.00
4,882,000	1918 S	2.50	5.50	9.50	25.00	50.00	200.00
8,362,000	1918 D	3.25	6.00	10.00	25.00	60.00	250.00
	1918 D over 7	225.00	275.00	465.00	850.00	1500.00	10,000.00
60,868,000	1919	.50	.65	1.25	3.00	7.50	35.00
7,521,000	1919 S	2.00	5.00	10.00	25.00	67.50	250.00
8,006,000	1919 D	3.00	6.00	15.00	35.00	72.50	300.00
63,093,000	1920	.40	.60	1.15	3.00	7.50	40.00
9,689,000	1920 S	1.50	2.50	16.00	25.00	50.00	250.00
9,418,000	1920 D	2.50	4.75	9.00	30.00	50.00	275.00
10,663,000	1921	.75	1.00	3.00	6.00	12.00	80.00
1,557,000	1921 S	8.00	15.00	30.00	70.00	110.00	450.00
35,715,000	1923	.40	.60	1.15	3.00	8.00	35.00
6,142,000	1923 S	1.50	2.50	6.00	20.00	45.00	200.00
21,620,000	1924	.40	.60	1.15	4.00	9.00	55.00
1,437,000	1924 S	4.00	6.00	14.00	65.00	140.00	750.00
5,258,000	1924 D	2.00	3.00	8.00	25.00	50.00	250.00
35,565,100	1925	.40	.60	1.15	3.00	6.50	35.00
6,256,000	1925 S	2.00	4.00	6.00	17.50	45.00	275.00
4,450,000	1925 D	3.25	5.25	12.00	35.00	55.00	275.00
44,693,000	1926	.40	.55	1.00	1.25	5.00	30.00
970,000	1926 S	6.00	8.00	15.00	45.00	150.00	600.00
5,638,000	1926 D	1.75	3.75	8.50	25.00	70.00	225.00
37,981,000	1927	.40	.55	1.00	1.25	5.00	25.00
3,430,000	1927 S	1.00	1.50	4.00	12.00	50.00	250.00
5,730,000	1927 D	.75	1.50	2.75	10.00	20.00	70.00

Quantity	Year	Good	Very Good	Fine	Very Fine	Ext. Fine	Unc.
23,411,000	1928	.35	.45	.75	2.00	4.00	27.50
6,936,000	1928 S	.60	.85	1.75	2.50	9.00	65.00
6,436,000	1928 D	·.55	.70	1.00	3.00	8.00	30.00
36,446,000	1929	.35	.50	.75	1.50	3.50	20.00
7,754,000	1929 S	.45	.55	.95	1.50	4.00	30.00
8,370,000	1929 D	.45	.65	1.00	2.00	4.00	30.00
22,849,000	1930	.35	.45	.75	1.50	3.50	25.00
5,435,000	1930 S	.60	.75	1.50	1.75	5.50	50.00
1,200,000	1931 S	3.50	4.00	5.00	6.00	12.50	65.00
20,213,000	1934	.30	.40	.65	1.50	3.50	25.00
7,480,003	1934 D	.45	.50	.75	1.50	4.00	35.00
58,264,000	1935	.30	.40	.50	.65	1.25	17.50
10,300,000	1935 S	.35	.40	.50	1.00	2.00	20.00
12,092,000	1935 D	.40	.45	.65	1.75	2.50	30.00
119,001,420	1936				.75	1.50	17.50
14,930,000	1936 S				.75	2.00	20.00
24,418,000	1936 D				.75	2.00	20.00
79,485,769	1937				.75	1.50	17.50
5,635,000	1937 S				.75	1.75	17.50
17,826,000 {	1937 D				.75	2.00	17.50
	1937 D three-legged buffalo				100.00	175.00	475.00
7,020,000	1938 D				1.25	1.75	17.50

HOW TO RECOGNIZE VARIETIES

The flat top and points of a "7" show above the upper loop of the "8" on the 1918/17 nickel. The upright of the "7" shows at the right inside edge of the upper loop and the left inside edge of the lower loop. The variety is found only on Denver mint issues.

Only one front leg shows clearly on the 1937 "3-legged" buffalo. The variety is found only on the Denver mint issue.

JEFFERSON NICKELS

The mint marks are to the right of the building or above it on the reverse until 1968, then on the obverse near the date.

Quantity	Year	Ext. Fine	Unc.
19,515,365	1938	$ .55	$1.50
4,105,000	1938 S	3.25	7.75
5,376,000	1938 D	2.25	6.00
120,627,535	1939	.35	1.35
6,630,000	1939 S	2.50	17.50
3,514,000	1939 D	9.00	55.00
176,499,158	1940	.35	.75
39,690,000	1940 S	.50	1.75
43,540,000	1940 D	.40	1.50
203,283,720	1941	.30	1.00
43,445,000	1941 S	.40	1.50
53,432,000	1941 D	.40	1.50
49,818,600	1942	.40	1.50
13,938,000	1942 D	2.00	15.00

Wartime Silver Content

Quantity	Year	Ext. Fine	Unc.
57,900.600	1942 P	4.00	15.00
32,900,000	1942 S	2.00	7.50
271,165,000	1943 P	1.25	3.25
104,060,000	1943 S	1.25	4.00
15,294,000	1943 D	2.50	4.25
119,150,000	1944 P	1.25	2.75
21,640,000	1944 S	1.50	5.00
32,309,000	1944 D	1.50	4.00
119,408,100	1945 P	1.25	3.00
58,939,000	1945 S	1.15	3.00
37,158,000	1945 D	1.15	3.00

Prewar Nickel Content

Quantity	Year	Unc.
161,116,000	1946	.50
13,560,000	1946 S	1.35
45,292,200	1946 D	.75
95,000,000	1947	.40
24,720,000	1947 S	1.25
37,822,000	1947 D	1.00
89,348,000	1948	.50
11,300,000	1948 S	1.50
44,734,000	1948 D	1.30
60,652,000	1949	.75
9,716,000	1949 S	2.75
35,238,000	1949 D	1.00
9,847,386	1950	2.50
2,630,030	1950 D	14.00
26,689,500	1951	1.10
7,776,000	1951 S	3.75
20,460,000	1951 D	2.00
64,069,980	1952	.55
20,572,000	1952 S	.85
30,638,000	1952 D	2.25
46,772,800	1953	.30
19,210,900	1953 S	.65
59,878,600	1953 D	.60

Quantity	Year	Unc.
47,917,350	1954	$.25
29,384,000	1954 S	.30
117,183,060	1954 D	.25

Quantity	Year	Unc.
8,266,200	1955	1.65
74,464,100	1955 D	.30
35,397,081	1956	.25
67,222,040	1956 D	.25
38,408,000	1957	.25
136,828,900	1957 D	.20
17,088,000	1958	.50
168,249,120	1958 D	.20
27,248,000	1959	.35
160,738,240	1959 D	.15
55,416,000	1960	.15
192,582,180	1960 D	.15
76,668,244	1961	.15
229,372,760	1961 D	.15
100,602,019	1962	.15
280,195,720	1962 D	.15
178,851,645	1963	.15
276,829,460	1963 D	.15
1,024,672,000	1964	.15
1,787,297,160	1964 D	.15
133,771,380	1965	.15
153,946,700	1966	.15
107,325,800	1967	.15
91,227,880	1968 D	.15
100,396,001	1968 S	.15
202,807,500	1969 D	.15
120,164,000	1969 S	.15
515,485,380	1970 D	.15
241,464,814	1970 S	.15
106,884,000	1971	.15
316,144,800	1971 D	.15
3,224,138	1971 S (proof only)	
202,036,000	1972	.15
351,694,600	1972 D	.15
3,267,667	1972 S (proof only)	
384,396,000	1973	.15
261,405,400	1973 D	.15
*2,769,624	1973 S (proof only)	
601,752,000	1974	.15
277,373,000	1974 D	.15
2,617,350	1974 S (proof only)	
181,772,000	1975	.15
401,875,300	1975 D	.15
	1975 S (proof only)	
367,124,000	1976	.15
563,964,147	1976 D	.15
	1976 S (proof only)	
585,376,000	1977	.15
297,313,422	1977 D	.15
	1977 S (proof only)	
391,308,000	1978	.15
313,092,780	1978 D	.15
	1978 S (proof only)	
	1979	.15
	1979 D	.15
	1979 S (proof only)	

Liberty Head Dime

UNCIRCULATED

The outline of the ribbon and the letters in LIBERTY are sharp. The leaves in the laurel wreath are clearly defined. There is a roundness to the cheek and features of the face.

EXTREMELY FINE

Traces of wear show on the cheek and on the lock of hair just above the eye.

FINE

Only partial LIBERTY is clear, TY especially being faint. The top outline of the ribbon and the outline of the laurel wreath are weak. The cheek has a decidedly flat appearance.

Liberty Head Dime

VERY GOOD

A much worn coin. LIB-
ERTY is completely worn
away except for a letter or
two. The bottom of the
laurel wreath, the curl in
front of the ear and the
eyebrow are all worn
smooth.

DIMES — LIBERTY HEAD TYPE

The mint marks are under the wreath on the reverse.

Quantity	Year	Good	Very Good	Fine	Very Fine	Ext. Fine	Unc.
12,121,245	1892........	$2.00	$3.75	$5.75	$10.00	$25.00	$185.00
3,841,700	1892 O....	4.50	8.00	10.00	17.50	30.00	200.00
990,710	1892 S.....	25.00	35.00	45.00	60.00	90.00	325.00
3,340,792	1893........	4.00	6.00	9.00	15.00	25.00	200.00
1,760,000	1893 O....	12.00	17.50	25.00	35.00	50.00	275.00
2,491,401	1893 S.....	5.50	7.00	13.50	20.00	35.00	275.00
1,330,972	1894........	7.00	10.00	15.00	25.00	35.00	225.00
720,000	1894 O....	30.00	42.50	70.00	100.00	175.00	750.00
24	1894 S ext. rare						100,000.00
690,880	1895........	35.00	50.00	80.00	100.00	150.00	450.00
440,000	1895 O....	80.00	110.00	160.00	220.00	325.00	1100.00
1,120,000	1895 S.....	13.50	20.00	27.50	40.00	65.00	350.00
2,000,762	1896........	5.50	8.00	12.50	20.00	32.50	215.00
610,000	1896 O...	40.00	50.00	70.00	90.00	150.00	

Quantity	Year	Good	Very Good	Fine	Very Fine	Ext. Fine	Unc.
575,056	1896 S	$32.50	$45.00	$65.00	$100.00	$150.00	$625.00
10,869,264	1897	1.50	2.25	5.50	8.00	20.00	175.00
666,000	1897 O	32.50	40.00	60.00	80.00	135.00	500.00
1,342,844	1897 S	7.50	13.50	22.50	37.50	60.00	275.00
16,320,735	1898	1.50	2.00	4.25	7.50	17.50	175.00
2,130,000	1898 O	4.00	6.25	12.50	27.50	55.00	250.00
1,702,507	1898 S	4.00	6.25	12.50	25.00	50.00	225.00
19,580,846	1899	1.35	1.75	4.25	10.00	20.00	165.00
2,650,000	1899 O	3.75	7.00	15.00	25.00	50.00	250.00
1,867,493	1899 S	4.00	6.50	12.50	20.00	40.00	1235.00
17,600,912	1900	1.25	2.00	5.00	7.00	17.50	125.00
2,010,000	1900 O	5.00	8.00	15.00	25.00	55.00	250.00
5,168,270	1900 S	2.00	3.25	6.00	10.00	22.50	150.00
18,860,478	1901	1.25	1.50	3.50	7.00	15.00	150.00
5,620,000	1901 O	1.85	3.25	7.00	15.00	40.00	375.00
593,022	1901 S	30.00	55.00	85.00	125.00	190.00	850.00
21,380,777	1902	1.25	2.00	4.25	10.00	20.00	175.00
4,500,000	1902 O	1.75	3.25	7.00	15.00	30.00	235.00
2,070,000	1902 S	3.50	7.00	12.50	25.00	50.00	275.00
19,500,755	1903	1.50	1.75	5.00	10.00	20.00	175.00
8,180,000	1903 O	1.75	2.75	6.50	12.50	27.50	225.00
613,300	1903 S	25.00	35.00	55.00	70.00	135.00	575.00
14,601,027	1904	1.35	1.75	5.25	10.00	25.00	175.00
800,000	1904 S	17.50	27.50	40.00	55.00	90.00	575.00
14,552,350	1905	1.25	1.50	5.00	10.00	17.50	175.00
3,400,000	1905 O	1.75	3.75	10.00	15.00	35.00	225.00
6,855,199	1905 S	1.50	2.50	5.50	12.00	25.00	225.00
19,958,406	1906	1.25	1.50	3.00	8.00	17.50	175.00
4,060,000	1906 D	1.50	2.50	7.00	12.50	25.00	185.00
2,610,000	1906 O	2.65	5.50	12.50	22.50	32.50	175.00
3,136,640	1906 S	2.00	3.75	7.50	12.50	30.00	175.00
22,220,575	1907	1.25	1.75	3.00	9.00	20.00	175.00
4,080,000	1907 D	1.50	3.50	7.00	12.50	30.00	175.00
5,058,000	1907 O	1.50	2.75	6.50	12.00	27.50	185.00
3,178,470	1907 S	1.50	2.75	7.00	12.50	27.50	185.00
10,600,545	1908	1.25	1.50	3.75	10.00	25.00	175.00
7,490,000	1908 D	1.25	1.75	3.50	9.00	22.50	175.00
1,789,000	1908 O	3.50	6.50	12.50	20.00	35.00	200.00
3,220,000	1908 S	1.50	2.75	7.00	12.00	25.00	180.00
10,240,650	1909	1.25	1.75	3.50	10.00	22.50	175.00
954,000	1909 D	3.75	6.50	14.00	27.50	50.00	225.00
2,287,000	1909 O	2.75	3.75	9.00	17.50	32.50	235.00
1,000,000	1909 S	4.25	7.75	17.50	35.00	55.00	235.00
11,520,551	1910	1.35	1.65	3.00	9.00	22.50	175.00
3,490,000	1910 D	1.65	2.50	5.00	11.00	27.50	200.00
1,240,000	1910 S	2.50	4.25	7.75	17.50	32.50	225.00
18,870,543	1911	1.25	1.75	3.00	7.50	22.50	175.00
11,209,000	1911 D	1.25	1.40	3.00	7.50	22.50	175.00
3,520,000	1911 S	1.50	2.25	3.75	11.00	27.50	185.00
19,350,700	1912	1.25	1.75	2.75	7.50	27.50	175.00
11,760,000	1912 D	1.35	1.75	2.75	7.50	27.50	175.00
3,420,000	1912 S	1.75	2.35	4.25	7.75	25.00	185.00
19,760,622	1913	1.25	1.65	2.75	6.75	22.50	175.00
510,000	1913 S	7.50	13.00	27.50	45.00	90.00	400.00
17,360,655	1914	1.25	1.75	2.75	7.50	22.50	175.00
11,908,000	1914 D	1.25	1.75	2.75	7.50	22.50	175.00
2,100,000	1914 S	1.75	2.75	7.00	11.00	27.50	185.00
5,620,450	1915	1.25	1.75	3.75	10.00	22.50	175.00
960,000	1915 S	2.50	3.25	10.00	16.50	32.50	190.00
18,490,000	1916	1.25	1.75	3.25	9.00	22.50	175.00
5,820,000	1916 S	1.25	1.75	3.25	9.00	22.50	175.00

Mercury Head Dime

UNCIRCULATED

Vertical rods in the fasces bundle are sharply out-lined. Diagonal and horizontal bands stand out clearly.

EXTREMELY FINE

The hair above the fore-head and in front of the ear show slight signs of wear. A spot of wear shows on the front of the wing.

VERY FINE

The vertical rods in the bundle have lost some of their clarity but are still visible. The horizontal bands show spots of wear.

Mercury Head Dime

GOOD

The vertical rods and the horizontal and diagonal bands are nearly smooth. The rim of the coin is flat.

DIMES — MERCURY HEAD TYPE

The mint marks are to the left of the fasces on the reverse.

Quantity	Year	Good	Very Good	Fine	Very Fine	Ext. Fine	Unc.
22,180,080	1916	$1.00	$1.50	$2.00	$3.25	$3.75	30.00
264,000	1916 D	190.00	250.00	375.00	575.00	875.00	2250.00
10,450,000	1916 S	2.75	3.75	5.50	7.00	13.50	37.50
55,230,000	1917	1.20	1.35	1.75	2.50	6.25	30.00
9,402,000	1917 D	2.15	4.50	7.75	12.00	30.00	150.00
27,330,000	1917 S	1.25	1.65	2.00	3.50	7.25	65.00
26,680,000	1918	1.10	1.35	3.75	7.50	20.00	70.00
22,674,800	1918 D	1.25	1.50	4.25	8.00	16.50	135.00
19,300,000	1918 S	1.10	1.35	2.35	7.00	16.50	125.00
35,740,000	1919	1.00	1.25	2.00	3.25	7.50	45.00
9,939,000	1919 D	1.75	3.00	8.00	15.00	32.50	190.00
8,850,000	1919 S	1.75	3.25	8.00	15.00	32.50	210.00
59,030,000	1920	1.00	1.50	1.50	1.75	4.00	30.00
19,171,000	1920 D	1.10	1.65	2.15	4.75	11.00	100.00
13,820,000	1920 S	1.10	1.25	2.00	4.50	12.00	100.00
1,230,000	1921	16.50	25.00	50.00	90.00	275.00	1250.00
1,080,000	1921 D	25.00	35.00	65.00	125.00	280.00	200.00
50,130,000	1923	1.00	1.10	1.20	1.50	3.50	25.00
6,440,000	1923 S	1.10	1.50	3.75	6.50	25.00	165.00
24,010,000	1924	1.00	1.10	1.25	2.00	5.00	50.00
6,810,000	1924 D	1.10	1.65	3.75	5.50	18.00	165.00
7,120,000	1924 S	1.00	1.35	2.50	5.50	18.00	160.00

MERCURY HEAD DIMES (continued)

Quantity	Year	Good	Very Good	Fine	Very Fine	Ext. Fine	Unc.
25,610,000	1925	1.00	1.15	1.35	2.00	5.00	50.00
5,117,000	1925 D	2.25	4.25'	9.00	22.50	70.00	425.00
5,850,000	1925 S	1.10	1.35	2.00	6.25	22.50	200.00
32,160,000	1926	1.00	1.15	1.30	1.50	4.00	25.00
6,828,000	1926 D	1.10	1.50	2.50	5.00	15.00	125.00
1,520,000	1926 S	6.50	8.50	16.50	22.50	65.00	700.00
28,080,000	1927	1.00	1.15	1.25	1.50	3.50	25.00
4,812,000	1927 D	1.15	2.75	5.50	20.00	35.00	300.00
4,770,000	1927 S	1.10	1.35	2.00	5.50	17.50	200.00
19,480,000	1928	1.00	1.15	1.25	1.50	3.50	35.00
4,161,000	1928 D	1.25	2.50	4.00	15.00	35.00	175.00
7,400,000	1928 S	1.10	1.25	1.50	3.75	11.00	100.00
25,970,000	1929	1.00	1.10	1.20	1.40	3.00	25.00
5,034,000	1929 D	1.10	1.25	2.40	3.25	6.50	30.00
4,730,000	1929 S	1.00	1.15	1.65	2.75	4.25	50.00
6,770,000	1930	1.00	1.15	1.50	1.75	4.50	40.00
1,843,000	1930 S	2.25	3.00	4.00	5.00	11.00	125.00
3,150,000	1931	1.20	1.30	1.75	3.25	7.25	60.00
1,260,000	1931 D	7.00	8.00	9.00	14.00	22.50	125.00
1,800,000	1931 S	2.25	3.50	4.00	4.75	12.	150.00
24,080,000	1934	1.00	1.15	1.35	1.40	4.00	32.50
6,772,000	1934 D	1.00	1.30	1.50	2.00	6.00	75.00
58,830,000	1935	$1.00	$1.10	$1.20	$1.30	$1.75	$20.00
10,477,000	1935 D	1.00	1.15	1.30	2.00	7.00	125.00
15,840,000	1935 S	1.00	1.10	1.20	1.30	2.25	30.00
87,504,130	1936				1.25	1.50	17.50
16,132,000	1936 D				1.35	5.00	60.00
9,210,000	1936 S				1.25	2.75	45.00
56,865,756	1937				1.00	1.50	12.00
14,146,000	1937 D				1.10	1.50	55.00
9,740,000	1937 S				1.10	1.50	40.00
22,198,728	1938				1.00	1.40	11.00
5,537,000	1938 D			.	1.25	2.25	35.00
8,090,000	1938 S				1.25	2.25	22.50
67,749,321	1939				1.10	1.65	.00
24,394,000	1939 D				1.10	1.65	12.50
10,540,000	1939 S				1.35	3.00	32.50
65,361,827	1940				1.10	1.50	9.00
21,198,000	1940 D				1.10	1.50	25.00
21,560,000	1940 S				1.10	1.50	16.50
175,106,557	1941				1.10	1.50	9.00
45,634,000	1941 D				1.10	1.50	25.00
43,090,000	1941 S				1.10	1.50	17.50
205,432,329 {	1942 over 1				250.00	325.00	1000.00
	1942						6.50
60,740,000	1942 D				1.10	1.50	15.00
49,300,000	1942 S				1.10	1.50	22.50
191,710,000	1943				1.10	1.50	7.00
71,949,000	1943 D				1.10	1.50	7.00
60,400,000	1943 S				1.10	1.50	11.00
231,410,000	1944				1.10	1.50	7.00
62,224,000	1944 D				1.10	1.50	7.00
49,490,000	1944 S				1.10	1.50	7.00
159,130,000	1945				1.10	1.50	7.00
40,245,000	1945 D				1.10	1.50	9.00
41,920,000	1945 S				1.10	1.50	9.00

The mint marks are at the left bottom of the torch on the reverse.

Quantity	Year	Ext. Fine	Unc.
255,250,000	1946	$1.15	$1.75
61,043,500	1946 D	1.15	2.00
27,900,000	1946 S	1.15	2.15
121,520,000	1947	1.15	1.85
46,835,000	1947 D	1.15	4.50
38,840,000	1947 S	1.15	3.75
74,950,000	1948		2.75
52,841,000	1948 D		2.75
35,520,000	1948 S		3.75
30,940,000	1949		15.00
26,034,000	1949 D		7.50
13,510,000	1949 S		32.50
50,181,500	1950		3.00
46,803,000	1950 D		2.25
20,440,000	1950 S		25.00
103,937,602	1951		2.50
52,191,800	1951 D		2.00
31,630,000	1951 S		12.50
99,122,073	1952		1.75
122,100,000	1952 D		1.75
44,419,500	1952 S		4.00
53,618,920	1953		2.00
136,400,000	1953 D		1.50
39,180,000	1953 S		1.50
114,243,503	1954		1.50
106,397,000	1954 D		1.50
22,860,000	1954 S		1.75
12,828,381	1955		1.75
13,959,000	1955 D		1.75
18,510,000	1955 S		1.50
108,821,081	1956		1.25
108,015,100	1956 D		1.25
160,160,000	1957		1.25
113,354,330	1957 D		1.25
31,910,000	1958		1.35
136,564,600	1958 D		1.15
85,780,000	1959		1.15
164,919,790	1959 D		1.15
70,390,000	1960		1.15
200,160,400	1960 D		1.15
96,758,244	1961		1.15
209,146,550	1961 D		1.15
75,668,019	1962		1.15
334,948,380	1962 D		1.15
126,725,645	1963		1.15
421,476,530	1963 D		1.15
929,360,000	1964		1.15
1,357,517,180	1964 D		1.15

Quantity	Year	Unc.
1,649,780,570	1965	$.25
1,380,474,957	1966	.25
2,244,007,320	1967	.25
424,470,400	1968	.25
480,748,280	1968 D	.25
3,041,509	1968 S (proof only)	
145,790,000	1969	.25
563,323,870	1969 D	.25
2,934,631	1969 S (proof only)	
345,570,000	1970	.25
754,942,100	1970 D	.25
2,632,810	1970 S (proof only)	
162,690,000	1971	.25
377,914,240	1971 D	.25
3,244,138	1971 S (proof only)	
431,540,000	1972	.25
330,290,000	1972 D	.25
3,267,667	1972 S (proof only)	
315,670,000	1973	.25
455,032,426	1973 D	.25
2,769,624	1973 S (proof only)	
470,248,000	1974	.25
571,083,000	1974 D	.25
2,617,350	1974 S (proof only)	
585,673,900	1975	.20
313,705,300	1975 D	.20
2,845,450	1975 S (proof only)	
568,760,000	1976	.20
695,222,774	1976 D	.20
4,149,730	1976 (proof only)	
796,930,000	1977	.20
376,607,228	1977 D	.20
3,251,152	1977 S (proof only)	
663,980,000	1978	.20
282,847,540	1978 D	.20
3,127,781	1978 S (proof only)	
	1979	.20
	1979 D	.20
	1979 S (proof only)	

Quarters

**Liberty Head
Quarter** *

UNCIRCULATED

Liberty's cap and hair, the laurel wreath and the LIBERTY
ribbon are well defined.

EXTREMELY FINE

Slight signs of wear show on the hair above the eye and
on the top fold of the cap.

* For reverses, see pp. 74-81.   **31**

VERY FINE

Definite areas of wear show on the forelock, cheek and laurel wreath. LIBERTY is clear but the bottom outline of the ribbon is weak.

FINE

Only partial LIBERTY is clear, RTY especially being faint. The top outline of the ribbon and the outline of the laurel wreath are vague.

          * For reverses, see pp. 74-81.

**Liberty Head
Quarter** *

VERY GOOD

LIBERTY is completely worn away except for a letter or two. Only a coarse outline of the laurel wreath remains.

GOOD

The head shows only in outline. No part of LIBERTY is visible. The rim is worn flat.

* For reverses, see pp. 74-81.

QUARTERS — LIBERTY HEAD (BARBER) TYPE

The mint marks are under the eagle on the reverse.

Quantity	Year	Good	Very Good	Fine	Very Fine	Ext. Fine	Unc.
8,237,245	1892	$3.00	$7.00	$10.00	$25.00	$55.00	$300.00
2,640,000	1892 O	6.00	10.00	12.00	30.00	60.00	325.00
964,079	1892 S	12.50	20.00	35.00	50.00	85.00	375.00
5,444,815	1893	2.50	5.25	10.00	25.00	55.00	300.00
3,396,000	1893 O	3.00	7.50	12.50	30.00	65.00	320.00
1,454,535	1893 S	7.00	11.00	16.00	37.50	70.00	350.00
3,432,972	1894	2.50	5.50	10.00	25.00	55.00	300.00
2,852,000	1894 O	3.25	7.50	14.00	27.50	65.00	320.00
2,648,821	1894 S	2.50	7.50	14.00	27.50	65.00	320.00
4,440,880	1895	2.50	5.00	10.00	25.00	55.00	300.00
2,816,000	1895 O	3.00	7.50	14.00	27.50	65.00	320.00
1,764,681	1895 S	6.00	10.00	16.00	32.50	65.00	320.00
3,874,762	1896	2.50	5.00	10.00	25.00	55.00	300.00
1,484,000	1896 O	5.00	10.00	25.00	40.00	85.00	700.00
188,039	1896 S	125.00	200.00	350.00	460.00	750.00	2750.00
8,140,731	1897	2.50	4.00	10.00	22.50	55.00	300.00
1,414,800	1897 O	7.00	11.00	20.00	40.00	80.00	600.00
542,229	1897 S	12.50	20.00	30.00	50.00	90.00	550.00
11,100,735	1898	2.50	4.00	10.00	20.00	50.00	300.00
1,868,000	1898 O	3.50	7.00	15.00	30.00	60.00	375.00
1,020,592	1898 S	6.00	10.00	16.00	30.00	55.00	475.00
12,624,846	1899	2.50	4.00	10.00	22.50	50.00	300.00
2,644,000	1899 O	3.00	5.00	12.00	27.50	55.00	375.00
708,000	1899 S	7.00	15.00	25.00	37.50	70.00	400.00
10,016,912	1900	2.50	4.00	10.00	22.50	55.00	300.00
3,416,000	1900 O	5.00	11.00	15.00	25.00	60.00	350.00
1,858,585	1900 S	2.50	5.00	12.50	22.50	50.00	350.00
8,892,813	1901	2.50	4.00	10.00	22.50	45.00	300.00
1,612,000	1901 O	10.00	17.50	40.00	70.00	135.00	550.00
72,664	1901 S	450.00	700.00	800.00	1200.00	1600.00	7500.00
12,197,744	1902	2.50	4.00	9.00	22.50	55.00	300.00
4,748,000	1902 O	2.75	4.50	14.00	25.00	60.00	325.00
1,524,612	1902 S	7.00	12.00	17.50	35.00	65.00	375.00
9,670,064	1903	2.75	4.50	10.00	22.50	55.00	300.00
3,500,000	1903 O	2.75	5.00	12.50	35.00	70.00	375.00
1,036,000	1903 S	7.00	12.00	25.00	55.00	70.00	425.00
9,588,813	1904	2.75	4.50	10.00	22.50	55.00	300.00
2,456,000	1904 O	5.00	9.00	16.50	30.00	75.00	500.00
4,968,250	1905	2.75	4.50	10.00	22.50	55.00	300.00
1,230,000	1905 O	5.50	12.00	20.00	40.00	65.00	375.00
1,884,000	1905 S	4.00	6.50	12.50	27.50	60.00	325.00
3,656,435	1906	2.75	5.00	10.00	22.50	60.00	300.00
3,280,000	1906 D	3.00	5.50	12.50	27.50	60.00	325.00
2,056,000	1906 O	5.00	9.00	14.00	32.50	65.00	325.00
7,192,575	1907	2.50	4.00	9.00	22.50	60.00	300.00
2,484,000	1907 D	3.50	6.50	12.50	27.50	60.00	325.00
4,560,000	1907 O	2.75	6.50	12.00	25.00	55.00	325.00
1,360,000	1907 S	3.50	6.50	12.50	27.50	65.00	325.00
4,232,545	1908	2.50	4.50	10.00	22.50	55.00	300.00
5,788,000	1908 D	2.50	4.50	10.00	22.50	55.00	325.00
6,244,000	1908 O	2.50	4.50	10.00	22.50	55.00	325.00
784,000	1908 S	7.00	14.00	17.50	35.00	75.0	475.00

Quantity	Year	Good	Very Good	Fine	Very Fine	Ext. Fine	Unc.
9,268,650	1909	$2.50	$3.50	$7.50	$25.00	$55.00	$300.00
5,114,000	1909 D	2.50	3.50	7.50	25.00	55.00	325.00
712,000	1909 O	10.00	17.50	35.00	70.00	125.00	800.00
1,348,000	1909 S	2.75	4.25	9.00	24.00	55.00	325.00
2,244,551	1910	2.50	3.50	9.00	24.00	55.00	300.00
1,500,000	1910 D	2.75	4.25	10.00	25.00	60.00	325.00
3,720,543	1911	2.50	3.50	9.00	24.00	55.00	300.00
933,600	1911 D	3.50	5.50	17.50	35.00	70.00	325.00
988,000	1911 S	3.50	4.25	12.50	25.00	65.00	325.00
4,400,700	1912	2.50	3.50	9.00	24.00	55.00	300.00
708,000	1912 S	3.50	6.00	14.00	30.00	70.00	400.00
484,613	1913	6.50	14.00	32.50	70.00	175.00	875.00
1,450,800	1913 D	3.50	4.25	12.50	32.50	65.00	300.00
40,000	1913 S	190.00	275.00	400.00	575.00	875.00	3000.00
6,244,610	1914	2.50	3.50	9.00	24.00	55.00	300.00
3,046,000	1914 D	2.50	3.50	9.00	24.00	55.00	300.00
264,000	1914 S	12.50	15.00	30.00	60.00	130.00	500.00
3,480,450	1915	2.50	3.50	9.00	24.00	55.00	300.00
3,694,000	1915 D	2.50	3.50	9.00	24.00	55.00	325.00
704,000	1915 S	3.00	5.00	12.50	27.50	60.00	375.00
1,788,000	1916	2.50	3.50	9.00	24.00	55.00	300.00
6,540,800	1916 D	2.50	3.50	9.00	24.00	55.00	325.00

Standing Liberty Quarter

UNCIRCULATED

Fine detail stands out on Liberty's chain mail shirt. The folds of her drapery and sash are distinct. The head often has a flat appearance even on uncirculated coins and, therefore, is not a significant grading factor. Specimens with rounded, full heads are especially desirable.

VERY FINE

Definite wear shows on the chain mail across Liberty's
breast. The fold of drapery across the right leg is smooth.

VERY GOOD

The body and the leg of Liberty are now quite flat. The
device on the shield is vague. Wear may extend into the
date but each digit must be discernible.

QUARTERS — STANDING LIBERTY TYPE

The mint marks are above and to the left of the date on the obverse.

1916-1917   1917-1930

Quantity	Year	Good	Very Good	Fine	Very Fine	Ext. Fine	Unc.
52,000	1916	$500.00	$700.00	$850.00	$1000.00	$1500.00	$2750.00
8,792,000	1917 type I*	7.50	10.00	15.00	25.00	55.00	250.00
1,509,200	1917 D type I*	7.50	11.00	17.50	27.50	60.00	275.00
1,952,000	1917 S type I*	7.50	11.00	17.50	27.50	60.00	275.00
13,880,000	1917 type II**	7.50	11.00	15.00	24.00	50.00	175.00
6,224,400	1917 Dtype II**	12.50	16.00	25.00	30.00	55.00	200.00
5,552,000	1917 S type II**	12.00	17.50	27.50	30.00	60.00	220.00
14,240,000	1918	7.00	10.00	14.00	20.00	40.00	165.00
7,380,000	1918 D	10.00	16.00	20.00	30.00	45.00	175.00
11,072,000	1918 S	7.00	10.00	15.00	22.50	40.00	140.00
?	1918 S over 17	300.00	400.00	600.00	850.00	1750.00	7000.00
11,324,000	1919	10.00	15.00	20.00	30.00	40.00	150.00
1,944,000	1919 D	30.00	45.00	55.00	85.00	125.00	385.00
1,836,000	1919 S	30.00	50.00	55.00	80.00	150.00	400.00
27,860,000	1920	5.50	8.00	10.00	15.00	27.50	125.00
3,586,400	1920 D	12.50	20.00	30.00	42.00	70.00	175.00
6,380,000	1920 S	8.00	11.00	15.00	25.00	40.00	140.00

QUARTERS — STANDING LIBERTY TYPE (continued)

Quantity	Year	Good	Very Good	Fine	Very Fine	Ext. Fine	Unc.
1,916,000	1921	$32.50	$45.00	$70.00	$90.00	$125.00	$365.00
9,716,000	1923	5.00	8.00	10.00	15.00	32.50	120.00
1,360,000	1923 S	45.00	60.00	80.00	100.00	165.00	425.00
10,920,000	1924	5.00	7.00	10.00	12.50	25.00	120.00
3,112,000	1924 D	16.00	24.00	30.00	40.00	50.00	120.00
2,860,000	1924 S	9.00	12.50	18.00	25.00	45.00	140.00
12,280,000	1925	3.00	4.00	4.50	9.00	25.00	100.00
11,316,000	1926	3.00	4.00	4.50	9.00	25.00	100.00
1,716,000	1926 D	3.25	4.00	7.00	14.00	35.00	115.00
2,700,000	1926 S	3.25	4.00	7.50	16.00	40.00	215.00
11,912,000	1927	3.00	4.00	4.50	9.00	25.00	100.00
976,400	1927 D	3.50	5.00	12.00	25.00	50.00	150.00
396,000	1927 S	7.00	8.50	22.50	55.00	200.00	1275.00
6,336,000	1928	3.00	4.00	4.50	9.00	22.50	100.00
1,627,600	1928 D	3.25	5.00	5.00	9.00	22.50	110.00
2,644,000	1928 S	3.00	4.00	4.75	9.00	22.50	110.00
11,140,000	1929	3.00	4.00	4.50	9.00	22.50	100.00
1,358,000	1929 D	3.25	4.50	6.00	9.00	25.00	120.00
1,764,000	1929 S	3.00	4.00	5.00	9.00	22.50	110.00
5,632,000	1930	3.00	4.00	5.00	9.00	22.50	100.00
1,556,000	1930 S	3.25	4.50	5.00	9.00	22.50	110.00

* stars at sides of eagle
** 3 stars below eagle

QUARTERS — WASHINGTON TYPE

The mint marks are under the eagle on the reverse.

Quantity	Year	Very Good	Fine	Very Fine	Ext. Fine	Unc.
5,404,000	1932	$3.25	$3.75	$4.00	$5.00	$35.00
436,800	1932 D	45.00	55.00	65.00	90.00	550.00
408,000	1932 S	45.00	50.00	55.00	70.00	275.00
31,912,052	1934	2.75	3.25	3.50	5.00	22.50
3,527,200	1934 D	2.50	5.50	8.00	20.00	125.00
32,484,000	1935	2.50	3.25	3.50	4.00	18.00
5,780,000	1935 D	2.75	3.75	8.00	15.00	125.00
5,660,000	1935 S	2.75	3.75	7.00	11.00	70.00
41,303,837	1936	2.50	3.00	3.25	3.75	20.00
5,374,000	1936 D	2.75	6.50	15.00	50.00	325.00
3,828,000	1936 S	2.50	3.00	3.75	10.00	100.00
19,701,542	1937	2.50	3.00	3.25	4.00	30.00
7,189,600	1937 D	2.50	3.00	3.50	5.00	55.00
1,652,000	1937 S	6.50	8.50	11.00	22.50	125.00
9,480,045	1938	2.50	3.00	6.50	14.00	55.00
2,832,000	1938 S	2.75	5.00	6.50	11.00	75.00
33,548,795	1939	2.50	3.25	3.50	4.50	15.00
7,092,000	1939 D	2.75	3.50	3.75	4.75	32.50
2,628,000	1939 S	3.00	3.50	4.50	11.00	55.00
35,715,246	1940	2.50	3.00	3.25	4.50	16.00
2,797,600	1940 D	2.75	3.75	6.50	14.00	80.00
8,244,000	1940 S	2.75	3.25	4.00	4.50	24.00
79,047,287	1941	2.50	3.00	3.75	4.00	7.50
16,714,800	1941 D	2.50	3.00	3.75	4.50	37.50
16,080,000	1941 S	2.50	3.00	3.75	4.50	35.00
102,117,123	1942			2.50	3.00	7.00
17,487,200	1942 D			2.75	4.00	24.00
19,384,000	1942 S			3.75	5.00	70.00
99,700,000	1943			2.50	3.75	7.50
16,095,600	1943 D			3.00	4.00	22.00
21,700,000	1943 S			3.00	4.00	32.50
104,956,000	1944			2.50	3.75	5.50
14,600,000	1944 D			2.50	3.75	8.50
12,560,000	1944 S			3.00	4.00	12.50
74,372,000	1945			2.50	3.75	8.00
12,341,600	1945 D			2.50	3.75	10.00
17,004,001	1945 S			2.50	3.75	9.00
53,436,000	1946			2.50	3.75	6.00
9,072,800	1946 D			2.50	3.75	12.50
4,204,000	1946 S			3.00	4.25	9.00
22,556,000	1947			2.50	3.75	7.00
15,338,400	1947 D			2.50	3.75	7.00
5,532,000	1947 S			2.75	4.25	9.00
35,196,000	1948			2.50	3.75	6.00
16,766,800	1948 D			2.50	3.75	7.00
15,960,000	1948 S			2.50	3.75	6.00
9,312,000	1949			5.00	6.00	20.00
10,068,400	1949 D			3.00	4.50	12.50
24,971,512	1950			2.50	3.75	5.00
21,075,600	1950 D			2.50	3.75	6.00
10,284,600	1950 S			2.50	3.75	9.00

WASHINGTON QUARTERS (continued)

Quantity	Year	Unc.
43,505,602	1951	5.50
35,354,800	1951 D	7.00
8,948,000	1951 S	15.00
38,862,073	1952	5.50
49,795,200	1952 D	5.00
13,707,800	1952 S	9.00
18,664,920	1953	5.50
56,112,400	1953 D	5.00
14,016,000	1953 S	8.00
54,645,503	1954	5.00
46,305,000	1954 D	5.00
11,834,722	1954 S	5.00
18,558,381	1955	5.50
3,182,400	1955 D	8.00
44,325,081	1956	3.50
32,334,500	1956 D	3.50
46,720,000	1957	3.50
77,924,160	1957 D	3.50
6,360,000	1958	5.00
78,124,900	1958 D	3.50
24,374,000	1959	3.50
62,054,232	1959 D	3.50
29,164,000	1960	3.50
63,000,324	1960 D	3.50
40,064,244	1961	3.50
83,656,928	1961 D	3.50
39,374,019	1962	3.50
127,554,756	1962 D	3.50
77,391,645	1963	3.50
135,288,184	1963 D	3.50

Quantity	Year	Unc.
570,390,585	1964	3.50
704,135,528	1964 D	3.50
1,817,357,540	1965	.75
818,836,911	1966	.75
1,524,031,848	1967	.75
220,731,500	1968	.75
101,534,500	1968 D	.90
3,041,509	1968 S (proof only)	

Quantity	Year	Unc.
176,212,000	1969	$ .60
114,372,000	1969 D	.75
2,934,631	1969 S (proof only)	
136,420,000	1970	.60
417,341,364	1970 D	.60
2,632,810	1970 S (proof only)	
109,284,000	1971	.60
258,634,428	1971 D	.60
3,224.138	1971 S (proof only)	
215,048,000	1972	.60
311,067,732	1972 D	.60
3,267,667	1972 S (proof only)	
346,924,000	1973	.60
232,977,400	1973 D	.60
2,796,624	1973 S (proof only)	
*	1974	.60
*	1974 D	.60
2,617,350	1974 S (proof only)	

* Mintage continued into 1975—struck simultaneously with Bicentennial coins dated 1776–1976.

809,784,016	1976 Copper-nickel clad	1.00
860,118,839	1976 D Copper-nickel clad	1.00
	1976 S copper-nickel clad (proof)	
*11,000,000	1976 S Silver clad	7.50
	1976 S Silver clad (proof)	

*Approximate mintage. Not all released.

468,556,000	1977	.50
256,524,978	1977 D	.50
	1977 S (proof only)	
521,452,000	1978	.50
287,373,152	1978 D	.50

1978 S (proof only)	
1979	.50
1979 D	.50
1979 S (proof only)	

Liberty Head Half

EXTREMELY FINE

Slight signs of wear show on the forelock of hair just above Liberty's brow and on the top fold of her cap.

The eagle's head, wing tips and the center tail feather show slight wear.

Liberty Head Half

FINE

LIBERTY is only partially clear, the last letters being particularly faint. The top outline of the ribbon and the outline of the laurel wreath are not distinct.

The reverse shows considerable wear. UNUM is faded on the ribbon, the lines in the shield are only partially visible, and the feathers on the eagle's legs are smooth.

HALF DOLLARS — LIBERTY HEAD (BARBER) TYPE

The mint marks are under the eagle on the reverse.

Quantity	Year	Good	Very Good	Fine	Very Fine	Ext. Fine	Unc.
935,245	1892	$8.00	$12.50	$30.00	$50.00	$130.00	$550.00
390,000	1892 O	70.00	80.00	120.00	190.00	250.00	700.00
1,029,028	1892 S	60.00	75.00	110.00	150.00	215.00	750.00
1,826,792	1893	8.00	12.50	30.00	50.00	130.00	550.00
1,389,000	1893 O	17.50	25.00	40.00	75.00	130.00	700.00
740,000	1893 S	45.00	65.00	90.00	135.00	190.00	750.00
1,148,972	1894	8.00	15.00	27.50	45.00	130.00	625.00
2,138,000	1894 O	8.00	15.00	30.00	50.00	140.00	700.00
4,048,690	1894 S	6.00	9.00	25.00	42.50	125.00	650.00
1,835,218	1895	6.00	9.00	27.50	42.50	125.00	600.00
1,766,000	1895 O	9.00	12.50	35.00	45.00	135.00	650.00
1,108,086	1895 S	15.00	25.00	27.50	60.00	135.00	650.00
950,762	1896	7.00	12.00	35.00	45.00	135.00	650.00
924,000	1896 O	15.00	20.00	35.00	65.00	150.00	700.00
1,140,948	1896 S	37.50	50.00	75.00	120.00	175.00	700.00
2,480,731	1897	6.50	9.00	17.50	40.00	160.00	700.00
632,000	1897 O	40.00	55.00	75.00	125.00	180.00	725.00
933,900	1897 S	40.00	60.00	80.00	135.00	190.00	750.00
2,956,735	1898	6.50	9.00	15.00	40.00	125.00	600.00
874,000	1898 O	12.00	17.50	35.00	50.00	160.00	700.00
2,358,550	1898 S	7.50	11.00	20.00	50.00	130.00	650.00
5,538,846	1899	5.50	7.50	15.00	37.50	120.00	550.00
1,724,000	1899 O	6.00	8.50	20.00	50.00	120.00	575.00
1,686,411	1899 S	9.00	12.50	25.00	50.00	120.00	600.00
4,762,912	1900	6.25	7.00	12.00	37.50	120.00	550.00
2,744,000	1900 O	6.25	7.50	12.50	40.00	130.00	600.00
2,560,322	1900 S	7.00	10.00	12.50	40.00	125.00	575.00
4,268,813	1901	6.25	7.50	12.00	37.50	115.00	500.00
1,124,000	1901 O	6.00	10.00	20.00	55.00	150.00	625.00
847,044	1901 S	11.00	20.00	50.00	110.00	225.00	1400.00
4,922,777	1902	6.25	7.50	12.50	37.50	115.00	525.00
2,526,000	1902 O	6.25	7.50	12.50	37.50	115.00	550.00
1,460,670	1902 S	6.25	8.00	15.00	40.00	115.00	550.00
2,278,755	1903	6.25	7.50	25.00	37.50	115.00	500.00
2,100,000	1903 O	6.25	7.50	17.50	37.50	115.00	500.00
1,920,772	1903 S	5.00	8.00	20.00	40.00	115.00	650.00
2,992,670	1904	5.50	7.00	12.50	37.50	115.00	500.00
1,117,600	1904 O	6.25	9.00	15.00	40.00	125.00	500.00
553,038	1904 S	11.00	20.00	37.50	80.00	180.00	700.00
662,727	1905	6.25	11.00	25.00	55.00	150.00	650.00
505,000	1905 O	10.00	17.50	35.00	70.00	165.00	525.00
2,494,000	1905 S	5.50	6.50	12.50	37.50	115.00	500.00

Quantity	Year	Good	Very Good	Fine	Very Fine	Ext. Fine	Unc.
2,638,675	1906	$6.25	$7.00	$12.50	37.50	$115.00	$525.00
4,028,000	1906 D	6.25	7.00	12.50	37.50	115.00	525.00
2,446,000	1906 O	6.25	7.00	12.50	37.50	115.00	525.00
1,740,154	1906 S	6.50	7.50	13.50	40.00	120.00	550.00
2,598,575	1907	6.25	7.00	12.50	37.50	115.00	525.00
3,856,000	1907 D	6.25	7.00	12.50	37.50	115.00	525.00
3,946,600	1907 O	6.25	7.00	12.50	37.50	115.00	525.00
1,250,000	1907 S	6.25	7.00	13.50	37.50	115.00	525.00
1,354,545	1908	6.25	7.00	13.50	37.50	115.00	525.00
3,280,000	1908 D	6.25	7.00	12.50	37.50	115.00	525.00
5,360,000	1908 O	6.25	7.00	12.50	37.50	115.00	525.00
1,644,828	1908 S	6.25	7.00	13.50	37.50	115.00	525.00
2,368,650	1909	6.25	7.00	12.50	37.50	115.00	525.00
925,400	1909 O	6.25	7.00	13.50	37.50	115.00	750.00
1,764,000	1909 S	6.25	7.00	12.50	37.50	115.00	525.00
418,551	1910	7.00	12.50	22.50	50.00	135.00	700.00
1,948,000	1910 S	6.25	7.00	12.50	37.50	115.00	525.00
1,406,543	1911	6.25	7.00	12.50	37.50	115.00	525.00
695,080	1911 D	6.25	7.00	14.00	40.00	115.00	575.00
1,272,000	1911 S	6.25	7.00	12.50	37.50	115.00	525.00
1,550,700	1912	6.25	7.00	12.50	37.50	115.00	525.00
2,300,800	1912 D	6.25	7.00	12.50	37.50	115.00	525.00
1,370,000	1912 S	6.25	7.00	12.50	37.50	115.00	525.00
188,627	1913	15.00	20.00	37.50	70.00	150.00	750.00
534,000	1913 D	6.25	8.00	12.50	45.00	115.00	575.00
604,000	1913 S	6.25	7.50	14.00	40.00	125.00	575.00
124,610	1914	25.00	30.00	50.00	90.00	190.00	900.00
992,000	1914 S	6.25	7.00	12.50	40.00	115.00	525.00
138,450	1915	18.00	25.00	45.00	80.00	150.00	875.00
1,170,400	1915 D	6.25	7.00	12.50	37.50	115.00	525.00
1,604,000	1915 S	6.25	7.00	12.50	37.50	115.00	525.00

HOW TO RECOGNIZE VARIETIES

The 1892 small "O" and regular "O" varieties are relative to one another. Two different size punches were used in putting the mint letter into dies of the same date.

Walking Liberty Half Dollar

VERY FINE

Wear is apparent across the breast and on the flowers in Liberty's arm. The lines in her drapery are faded.

There is a definite area of wear on the eagle's breast and on the tip of the wing.

VERY GOOD

All fine detail is gone from the eagle's body. The claws grasping the branch are no longer distinct.

A much worn coin in this condition. Liberty is visible only in outline. Wear shows also in the field of the flag.

HALF DOLLARS — WALKING LIBERTY TYPE

The mint marks are to the left of "half dollar" on the reverse.

Quantity	Year	Good	Very Good	Fine	Very Fine	Ext. Fine	Unc.
608,000	1916	$12.00	$22.50	$35.00	$65.00	$110.00	$325.00
1,014,400	1916 D on obv	7.00	11.00	20.00	40.00	85.00	285.00
508,000	1916 S on obv	30.00	35.00	70.00	130.00	235.00	550.00
12,992,000	1917	6.50	7.50	9.00	12.50	27.50	120.00
765,400	1917 D on obv	7.00	11.00	32.50	55.00	110.00	350.00
1,940,000	1917 D on rev	6.50	7.50	17.50	35.00	90.00	400.00
952,000	1917 S on obv	8.00	12.00	35.00	90.00	200.00	700.00
5,554,000	1917 S on rev	6.50	7.50	9.00	15.00	37.50	275.00
6,634,000	1918	6.50	7.50	7.50	20.00	90.00	300.00
3,853,040	1918 D	6.50	8.00	8.50	35.00	100.00	500.00
10,282,000	1918 S	6.50	7.50	7.50	17.50	70.00	325.00
962,000	1919	7.00	9.00	20.00	85.00	200.00	1000.00
1,165,000	1919 D	7.00	9.00	20.00	100.00	275.00	1500.00
1,552,000	1919 S	6.50	7.50	18.00	75.00	240.00	2000.00
6,372,000	1920	6.50	7.00	10.00	17.50	45.00	250.00
1,551,000	1920 D	6.50	7.50	12.50	70.00	150.00	1200.00
4,624,000	1920 S	6.50	7.50	12.00	35.00	80.00	1100.00
246,000	1921	40.00	55.00	90.00	220.00	500.00	1800.00
208,000	1921 D	65.00	80.00	125.00	225.00	625.00	2000.00
548,000	1921 S	8.00	12.50	27.50	135.00	500.00	7500.00
2,178,000	1923 S	6.50	7.00	9.00	40.00	110.00	900.00
2,392,000	1927 S	6.50	7.00	9.00	25.00	65.00	650.00
1,940,000	1928 S		6.50	7.00	25.00	90.00	750.00
1,001,200	1929 D		7.00	8.00	20.00	45.00	275.00
1,902,000	1929 S		6.50	7.00	12.50	40.00	275.00
1,786,000	1933 S		6.50	7.00	17.50	50.00	400.00
6,964,000	1934		6.50	7.00	9.00	11.00	60.00
2,361,400	1934 D		6.50	7.50	10.00	30.00	225.00
3,652,000	1934 S		6.50	7.00	8.00	25.00	300.00
9,162,000	1935		6.50	7.00	8.00	10.00	45.00
3,003,800	1935 D		6.50	7.00	7.50	25.00	210.00
3,854,000	1935 S		6.50	7.00	7.50	30.00	285.00
12,617,901	1936		6.50	7.00	7.50	10.00	45.00
4,252,400	1936 D		6.50	7.00	8.00	15.00	120.00
3,884,000	1936 S		6.50	7.00	8.00	20.00	200.00
9,527,728	1937		6.50	7.00	7.50	9.00	45.00
1,760,001	1937 D		6.50	7.00	8.00	27.50	225.00
2,090,000	1937 S		6.50	7.00	7.50	20.00	200.00
4,118,152	1938		6.50	7.50	8.00	12.50	90.00
491,600	1938 D		27.50	30.00	37.50	75.00	450.00
6,820,808	1939		6.50	7.00	7.50	8.00	50.00
4,267,800	1939 D		6.50	7.00	7.50	8.50	50.00
2,552,000	1939 S		6.50	7.00	7.50	15.00	90.00
9,167,279	1940				6.50	7.50	45.00
4,550,000	1940 S				6.50	10.00	55.00
24,207,412	1941				6.50	8.00	40.00

Quantity	Year	Good	Very Good	Fine	Very Fine	Ext. Fine	Unc.
11,248,400	1941 D				6.50	8.50	50.00
8,098,000	1941 S				8.00	15.00	120.00
47,839,120	1942				6.50	8.00	40.00
10,973,800	1942 D				7.50	10.00	50.00
12,708,000	1942 S				7.50	12.50	90.00
53,190,000	1943				6.50	8.00	40.00
11,346,000	1943 D				6.50	9.00	50.00
13,450,000	1943 S				6.50	8.50	45.00
28,206,000	1944				6.50	7.50	35.00
9,769,000	1944 D				6.50	9.00	50.00
8,904,000	1944 S				6.50	9.00	55.00
31,502,000	1945				6.50	8.00	35.00
9,966,800	1945 D				6.50	9.00	60.00
10,156,000	1945 S				6.50	9.00	60.00
12,118,000	1946				6.50	9.00	50.00
2,151,100	1946 D				6.50	9.00	60.00
3,724,000	1946 S				6.50	9.00	70.00
4,094,000	1947				6.50	9.00	55.00
3,900,000	1947 D				6.50	9.00	55.00

The mint marks are above the Liberty Bell on the reverse.

Quantity	Year	Very Fine	Ext. Fine	Unc.
3,006,814	1948	$6.50	$7.50	$30.00
4,028,600	1948 D	6.50	7.50	25.00
5,714,000	1949	6.50	8.00	60.00
4,120,600	1949 D	6.50	8.00	50.00
3,744,000	1949 S	7.00	11.00	70.00
7,793,509	1950	6.50	7.50	55.00
8,031,600	1950 D	6.50	7.50	35.00
16,859,602	1951	6.50	7.50	20.00
9,475,200	1951 D	6.50	7.50	30.00
13,696,000	1951 S	6.50	7.50	22.00
21,274,073	1952	6.50	7.50	15.00
25,395,600	1952 D	6.50	7.50	11.00
5,526,000	1952 S	6.50	7.50	35.00
2,796,920	1953	6.50	8.00	18.00
20,900,400	1953 D	6.50	7.50	11.00
4,148,000	1953 S	6.50	7.50	20.00
13,421,503	1954	6.50	7.50	10.00
25,445,580	1954 D	6.50	7.50	10.00
4,993,400	1954 S	6.50	7.50	11.00
2,876,381	1955	6.50	9.00	15.00

Quantity	Year	Ext. Fine	Unc.	Quantity	Year	Ext. Fine	Unc.
4,213,081	1956	$6.50	$7.50	18,215,812	1960 D	$6.50	$7.50
5,150,000	1957	6.50	7.50	11,318,244	1961	6.50	7.50
19,966,850	1957 D	6.50	7.50	20,276,442	1961 D	6.50	7.50
4,042,000	1958	6.50	7.50	12,932,019	1962	6.50	7.50
23,962,412	1958 D	6.50	7.50	70,473,281	1962 D	6.50	7.50
6,200,000	1959	6.50	7.50		1963	6.50	7.50
13,053,750	1959 D	6.50	7.50		1963 D	6.50	7.50
6,024,000	1960	6.50	7.50				

HALF DOLLARS—KENNEDY TYPE

The mint marks are near the claw holding the laurel wreath on the reverse.

Quantity	Year	Unc.	Quantity	Year	Unc.
273,304,004	1964	$7.50	3,267,667	1971 S (proof only)	
156,205,446	1964 D	7.50	153,180,000	1972	$2.00
63,519,366	1965	4.00	141,890,000	1972 D	2.00
106,723,349	1966	3.75	3,267,667	1972 S (proof only)	
295,046,978	1967	3.75	64,964,000	1973	2.00
246,951,930	1968 D	3.75	83,171,400	1973 D:	2.00
3,041,509	1968 S (proof only)		2,769,624	1973 S (proof only)	
129,881,800	1969 D	3.75	*	1974	2.00
2,934,631	1969 S (proof only)		*	1974 D	2.00
2,150,000	1970 D	40.00	2,617,350	1974 S (proof only)	
2,632,810	1970 S (proof only)				
155,164,000	1971	2.00			
302,097,424	1971 D	2.00			

* Mintage continued into 1975—struck simultaneously with Bicentennial coins dated 1776–1976.
Mintage of Bicentennial coins dated 1776–1976 began in March 1975.

Quantity	Year	Unc.	Quantity	Year	Unc.
234,308,000	1976 Copper-nickel clad	1.50	43,598,000	1977	1.00
287,565,248	1976 D Copper-nickel clad	1.50	31,449,106	1977 D	1.00
	1976 S Copper-nickel clad (proof)			1977 S (proof only)	
			14,350,000	1978	1.00
			13,765,799	1978 D	1.00
				1978 S (proof only)	
*4,239,722	1976 S Silver clad	15.00			
	1976 S Silver clad (proof)			1979	1.00
				1979 D	1.00
				1979 S (proof only)	

*Approximate mintage. Not all released.

Liberty Head Silver Dollar

EXTREMELY FINE

The first slight signs of wear appear in the hair above the forehead.

Traces of wear show on the highest part of the eagle's breast.

FINE

Considerable wear shows in the hair. There are smooth spots in the hair below the ear and at the back of the neck.

Liberty Head Silver Dollar

FINE

The eagle's legs and tail feathers have worn spots. The breast and head are worn quite smooth.

The mint mark is on the reverse under the eagle.

Quantity	Year	Fine	Very Fine	Ext. Fine	Unc.
	1878 8 feathers	$13.50	$15.00	$17.50	$60.00
10,509,550	1878 7 feathers		13.50	15.00	40.00
	1878 7 over 8 feathers	18.50	25.00	28.00	65.00
9,774,000	1878 S		15.00	16.50	40.00
2,212,000	1878 CC	16.00	26.00	35.00	100.00
14,807,100	1879		13.50	14.00	35.00
2,887,000	1879 O	14.00	15.00	16.50	70.00
9,110,000	1879 S		13.50	14.00	40.00
756,000	1879 CC	35.00	75.00	225.00	950.00
12,601,355	1880		13.50	14.00	35.00
5,305,000	1880 O	13.50	14.00	16.00	100.00
8,900,000	1880 S		13.50	15.00	30.00
591,000	1880 CC	40.00	60.00	75.00	100.00
9,163,975	1881		13.50	15.00	30.00
5,708,000	1881 O	13.50	15.00	16.00	30.00
12,760,000	1881 S	13.50	15.00	16.00	30.00
296,000	1881 CC	70.00	80.00	100.00	175.00
11,101,100	1882		13.50	15.00	35.00
6,090,000	1882 O	13.50	15.00	16.00	35.00
9,250,000	1882 S		13.50	15.00	35.00
1,133,000	1882 CC	25.00	30.00	35.00	100.00
12,291,039	1883		13.50	15.00	35.00
8,725,000	1883 O		13.50	14.00	16.00
6,250,000	1883 S	15.00	16.50	25.00	300.00
1,204,000	1883 CC	25.00	30.00	35.00	70.00
14,070,875	1884		14.00	15.00	55.00
9,730,000	1884 O		13.50	14.00	27.50
3,200,000	1884 S	15.00	16.50	20.00	1250.00
1,136,000	1884 CC	30.00	35.00	40.00	75.00
17,787,767	1885		13.50	15.00	30.00
9,185,000	1885 O		13.50	15.00	27.50
1,497,000	1885 S	15.00	17.50	27.50	115.00
228,000	1885 CC	115.00	125.00	135.00	200.00
19,963,886	1886		13.50	14.00	32.50
10,710,000	1886 O	14.00	15.00	17.50	350.00
750,000	1886 S	20.00	24.00	28.00	200.00
20,290,710	1887		13.50	14.00	30.00
11,550,000	1887 O	14.00	15.00	16.00	55.00
1,771,000	1887 S	15.00	17.50	25.00	120.00
19,183,833	1888		13.50	15.00	30.00
12,150,000	1888 O	14.00	15.00	17.50	35.00
657,000	1888 S	25.00	27.50	35.00	300.00

DOLLARS — LIBERTY HEAD (MORGAN) TYPE (continued)

Quantity	Year	Fine	Very Fine	Ext. Fine	Unc.
21,726,811	1889		$14.00	$15.00	$30.00
11,875,000	1889 O	$13.50	15.00	17.50	150.00
700,000	1889 S	22.50	24.00	32.50	180.00
350,000	1889 CC	140.00	200.00	475.00	5000.00
16,802,590	1890		13.50	15.00	45.00
10,701,000	1890 O	13.50	15.00	16.00	80.00
8,230,373	1890 S	13.50	15.00	17.50	90.00
2,309,041	1890 CC	25.00	30.00	35.00	215.00
8,694,206	1891	14.00	16.00	17.50	180.00
7,954,529	1891 O	14.00	16.00	17.50	190.00
5,296,000	1891 S	14.00	16.50	17.50	100.00
1,618,000	1891 CC	25.00	30.00	35.00	175.00
1,037,245	1892	15.00	17.50	25.00	135.00
2,744,000	1892 O	15.00	17.50	25.00	215.00
1,200,000	1892 S	18.00	30.00	150.00	13,000.00
1,352,000	1892 CC	30.00	50.00	110.00	415.00
378,792	1893	45.00	55.00	75.00	400.00
300,000	1893 O	50.00	90.00	175.00	1250.00
100,000	1893 S	650.00	900.00	3000.00	30,000.00
677,000	1893 CC	50.00	95.00	280.00	1050.00
110,972	1894	200.00	350.00	475.00	1000.00
1,723,000	1894 O	15.00	17.50	35.00	650.00
1,260,000	1894 S	17.50	22.50	75.00	375.00
12,880	1895 rare				
450,000	1895 O	60.00	90.00	175.00	2100.00
400,000	1895 S	80.00	150.00	375.00	2000.00
9,976,762	1896	13.50	15.00	17.50	37.50
4,900,000	1896 O	14.00	16.00	25.00	450.00
5,000,000	1896 S	15.00	25.00	80.00	750.00
2,822,731	1897	14.00	15.00	17.50	40.00
4,004,000	1897 O	14.00	15.00	18.00	365.00
5,825,000	1897 S	14.00	16.00	18.00	90.00
5,884,735	1898	14.00	15.00	17.50	37.50
4,440,000	1898 O	14.00	15.00	17.50	32.50
4,102,000	1898 S	15.00	17.50	20.00	365.00
330,846	1899	30.00	35.00	45.00	125.00
12,290,000	1899 O		14.00	16.00	32.50
2,562,000	1899 S	14.00	16.50	30.00	425.00
8,830,912	1900		14.00	16.00	35.00
12,590,000	1900 O		14.00	16.00	35.00
3,540,000	1900 S	15.00	18.00	25.00	140.00
6,962,813	1901	17.50	25.00	40.00	1000.00
13,320,000	1901 O		14.00	16.00	35.00
2,284,000	1901 S	15.00	18.00	25.00	320.00
7,994,777	1902	14.00	16.00	17.50	70.0
8,636,000	1902 O		14.00	16.00	30.00
1,530,000	1902 S	32.50	50.00	75.00	250.00
4,652,755	1903	15.00	17.50	22.50	70.00
4,450,000	1903 O	90.00	125.00	140.00	300.00
1,241,000	1903 S	18.00	25.00	125.00	1600.00
2,788,650	1904	15.00	17.50	20.00	200.00
3,720,000	1904 O	14.00	16.00	18.00	30.00
2,304,000	1904 S	16.00	22.50	75.00	850.00
44,690,000	1921			14.00	20.00
21,695,000	1921 S			14.00	70.00
20,345,000	1921 D			14.00	45.00

53

Peace Dollar

EXTREMELY FINE

The first sign of wear shows on the lock of hair crossing over the band of the coronet and in the hair above Liberty's ear.

Traces of wear show at the top and along the front edge of the eagle's closest wing.

The mint marks are at the bottom to the left of the eagle's wing on the reverse.

Quantity	Year	Ext. Fine	Unc.	Quantity	Year	Ext. Fine	Unc.
1,006,473	1921	$40.00	$275.00	2,348,700	1926 D....	16.00	135.00
51,737,000	1922	15.00	24.00	6,980,000	1926 S	16.00	50.00
15,063,000	1922 D....	15.00	40.00	848,000	1927	30.00	80.00
17,475,000	1922 S	15.00	40.00	1,268,900	1927 D....	25.00	300.00
30,800,000	1923	15.00	20.00	866,000	1927 S	25.00	325.00
6,811,000	1923 D....	15.00	60.00	360,649	1928	200.00	375.00
19,020,000	1923 S	15.00	100.00	1,632,000	1928 S	15.00	225.00
11,811,000	1924	15.00	20.00	954,057	1934	25.00	80.00
1,728,000	1924 S	20.00	130.00	1,569,000	1934 D....	20.00	110.00
10,198,000	1925	15.00	20.00	1,011,000	1934 S	115.00	1750.00
1,610,000	1925 S.....	20.00	210.00	1,576,000	1935	20.00	65.00
1,939,000	1926	16.50	40.00	1,964,000	1935 S	25.00	165.00

SILVER DOLLARS — EISENHOWER TYPE

Quantity	Year	Unc.
	1971........................	$1.50
	1971 D	1.50
	1971 S	3.50

DOLLARS — EISENHOWER TYPE (continued)

Quantity	Year	Unc.	Quantity	Year	Unc.
47,799,000	1971..........	$2.50	2,000,056	1973..........	25.00
68,587,424	1971 D	2.35	2,000,000	1973 D	25.00
6,668,526	1971 S	9.00	1,883,140	1973 S.......	16.00
75,890,000	1972..........	2.50	27,366,000	1974..........	2.35
95,548,511	1972 D	2.35	35,466,000	1974 D	2.35
2,193,056	1972 S	16.00	1,900,000	1974 S.......	17.50

4,019,000	1976 Copper-nickel clad, Variety I	$8.00
113,318,000	1976 Copper-nickel clad, Variety II	5.00
21,048,710	1976 D Copper-nickel clad, Variety I	6.00
82,179,564	1976 D Copper-nickel clad, Variety II	5.00
	1976 S Copper-nickel clad, Variety I (proof)	
	1976 S Copper-nickel clad, Variety II (proof)	
	1976 S Silver clad, Variety I (proof)	
*4,149,730	1976 S Silver clad, Variety I	17.50
12,596,000	1977	2.00
32,983,006	1977 D	2.00
	1977 S (proof only)	
25,702,000	1978	2.00
23,012,890	1978 D	2.00
	1978 S (proof only)	

DOLLARS—SUSAN B. ANTHONY TYPE

1979		1.50
1979 D		1.50
1979 S		1.50

Note: Proofs also struck at San Francisco.

3. THE DESIGNERS OF U.S. COINS

A TABLE OF THE DESIGNERS OF U.S. COINS, LOCATION OF THEIR INITIALS ON THE COINAGE.

Flying Eagle designed by Christian Gobrecht and adapted for the cent by James B. Longacre, no initial.

Indian Head cent designed by James B. Longacre, "L" on ribbon below feathers of the headdress.

Lincoln cent designed by Victor D. Brenner, "VDB" on reverse at bottom (1909) or on truncation of the bust (1918-date). Memorial reverse designed by Frank Gasparro, "FG" at lower right corner of building.

Shield nickel designed by James B. Longacre, no intial.

Liberty head nickel designed by Charles E. Barber, no initial.

Buffalo nickel designed by James E. Fraser, "F" below the date on obverse.

Jefferson nickel designed by Felix Schlag, no initial.

Liberty head dime designed by Charles E. Barber, "B" on truncation of neck.

Mercury head dime designed by A. A. Weinman, "AW" in field back of the neck.

Roosevelt dime designed by John R. Sinnock, "JS" at truncation of neck.

Liberty head quarter designed by Charles E. Barber, "B" at base of neck.

Standing Liberty quarter designed by Herman A. MacNeil, "M" above and to the right of date.

Washington quarter designed by John Flanagan, "JF" at base of neck.

Liberty head half dollar designed by Charles E. Barber, "B" at base of neck.

Walking Liberty half dollar designed by A. A. Weinman, "AW" in field at lower right on the reverse.

Franklin half dollar designed by John R. Sinnock, "JRS" below shoulder.

Liberty head dollar designed by George T. Morgan, "M" on truncation of the bust.

Peace dollar designed by Anthony de Francisci, "AF" in monogram appears in field under the neck.

4. THE IMPORTANCE OF
MINT MARKS

Mint marks are extremely important when we are determining the value of a coin. These marks are small letters struck on a coin to indicate the mint that issued it. At one time or another the United States has had seven mints, only two of which are still in operation.

Here is a list of our mints, their years of operation, and the mint mark used to identify their coins:

Mint	Years	Mint Mark
Philadelphia, Pa.	1792 to date	none
Dahlonega, Ga.	1838-1861	D
Charlotte, N. C.	1838-1861	C
New Orleans, La.	1838-1909	O
San Francisco, Cal.	1854-1955	S
Carson City, Nev	1870-1893	CC
Denver, Colo.	1906 to date	D

As you see, if a coin has no mint mark it has been struck at Philadelphia. (There is one exception to this rule. The wartime Jefferson nickels of this mint had a P mint mark indicating a change in the composition of the metal.) Coins produced at any of the branch mints have a letter on them showing where they are from.

Recognizing these mint marks is important because when a coin is issued by two or more mints in the same year there is often a considerable difference in the quantities issued by each mint. When there is a great variation in the number of coins issued, it is very likely that there will be a sizable variation in price. Take the catalogue value of the 1913 quarters. Here are the values in "Uncirculated" condition:

Quantity	Mint	Mint Mark	Value
484,613	Philadelphia	none	$ 95.00
1,450,800	Denver	D	52.50
40,000	San Francisco	S	1,100.00

To have this important information about each coin, we need to find the mint mark on the coin, as shown in the following pictures and table.

Indian Head Cents: on the reverse, at the bottom under the wreath.

Lincoln Head Cents: on the obverse, under the date.

Three Cents — Silver: on the reverse, to the right of the "III."

Liberty Head Nickels: on the reverse, to the left of "cents."

Buffalo Nickels: on the reverse, under "Five cents."

Jefferson Nickels: on the reverse, to the right of the building, or above it.

Liberty Seated Half Dimes: on the reverse, under the wreath, or within it.

Liberty Seated Dimes: on the reverse, under the wreath, or within it.

Liberty Head Dimes: on the reverse, under the wreath.

Mercury Head Dimes: on the reverse, to the left of the fasces.

Roosevelt Dimes: on the reverse, at the left bottom of the torch.

Twenty Cent Pieces: on the reverse, under the eagle.

Liberty Seated Quarters: on the reverse, under the eagle.

Liberty Head Quarters: on the reverse, under the eagle.

Standing Liberty Quarters: on the obverse, above and to the left of the date.

Washington Quarters: on the reverse, under the eagle.

Bust Type Half Dollars: on the obverse, above the date.

Liberty Seated Half Dollars: on the reverse, under the eagle.

Liberty Head Half Dollars: on the reverse, under the eagle.

Walking Liberty Half Dollars: on the obverse, below "In God We Trust," or on the reverse, below branch at lower left.

Franklin Half Dollars: on the reverse, above the Liberty Bell.

Kennedy Half Dollars: on the reverse.

Liberty Seated Dollars: on the reverse, under the eagle.

Liberty Head Dollars: on the reverse, under the eagle.

Peace Dollars: on the reverse, at the bottom, to the left of the eagle's wing.

Trade Dollars: on the reverse, under the eagle.

(Above) The mint mark on the Indian Head Cent (enlarged) appears on the reverse at the bottom under the wreath. (Below) The mint mark on the Lincoln Head Cent (enlarged) appears on the obverse under the date.

(Above) The mint mark on the Liberty Head Nickel (enlarged) appears on the reverse, to the left of "cents." (Below) The mint mark on the Buffalo (or Indian Head) Nickel (enlarged) appears on the reverse, under "Five cents."

The mint mark on Jefferson Nickels (enlarged) appears to the right of the building (above) or, on wartime issues, just above the building (below).

(Above) The mint mark on the Liberty Head Dime (enlarged) appears on the reverse, under the wreath. (Below) The mint mark on the Mercury Head Dime (enlarged) appears on the reverse, to the left of the fasces.

(Above) The mint mark on the Roosevelt Dime (enlarged) appears on the reverse, at the left bottom of the torch. (Below) The mint mark on the Liberty Head Quarter appears on the reverse, under the eagle.

(Above) The mint mark on the Standing Liberty Quarter (enlarged) appears above and to the left of the date. (Below) The mint mark on the Washington Quarter (enlarged) appears under the eagle.

The mint mark on the Liberty Head Half Dollar (enlarged) appears on the reverse, under the eagle.

The mint mark on the Walking Liberty Half Dollar (enlarged) appears on the reverse below the branch and to the left of "half dollar" on the late 1917 and all following dates. The mint mark appears below "In God We Trust" on the obverse of the 1916 and early 1917 issues.

The mint mark on the Franklin Half Dollar (enlarged) appears on the reverse, above the Liberty Bell.

The mint mark on the Liberty Head Dollar (enlarged) appears on the reverse, under the eagle.

The mint mark on the Liberty Head Dollar (enlarged) appears on the reverse, under the eagle.

5. HOW TO DETERMINE A COIN'S CONDITION

The importance of mint marks in coin evaluation was demonstrated in the last chapter. Since there is usually a significant difference in the number of pieces struck at each mint, you must be able to recognize mint marks and know exactly which issue you have. When you look for your coin in the catalogue listings you will see there is another factor that affects a coin's value—its condition.

Have you ever noticed how people react to the condition of coins? They take a childlike pleasure in a bright, clear, shiny, sharply outlined coin. Even if it's only a penny, they find something festive and cheerful about a coin when it's brand-new—just put into circulation.

On the other hand, a worn, faded, tired-looking coin, even if it's worth fifty times the value of a shiny penny, evokes no emotional reaction at all. We part with it readily, whereas disposing of the shiny new penny costs us something of a pang.

Well, the man who feels that slight tinge of regret is really akin to the coin collector, who loves coins for their own sake. The physical state of coins—*their condition*—is tremendously important to the collector. A coin in splendid condition is a desirable coin—a miniature work of art. It is likely to be worth considerably more than its face value. But a worn, faded coin is depressingly close to an anonymous metal disc, totally lacking in distinctive character.

Grading coins

Since there is a price tag on the different kinds of conditions, it is important for the collector to be able to grade coins accurately. In buying, selling or trading coins there is often more dispute over grading than price. Collectors and dealers use terms such as "Very Fine" to describe the state of preservation of their coins. Grading is the process of assigning the proper label to a given coin.

Condition standards

Here are the accepted standards for each condition:

UNCIRCULATED (Unc.) In new condition. All lettering, the date and details of the design are extremely clear. In the modern minting process, coins slide down chutes and are packed and shipped loose in bags. Even an uncirculated coin may show a few light scratches, or abrasions, or scuff marks from this rough handling. An uncirculated coin, however, shows no sign of wear or serious damage at any point. An absolutely perfect coin is often described as Gem Uncirculated or FDC (Fleur de Coin). Uncirculated coins are often brilliant but not necessarily so.

EXTREMELY FINE (EF or XF) Similar to Uncirculated except that the very highest points of the design show the slightest signs of wear or rubbing. The first point of wear is given in the text for each different design coin. All fine detail is still clear and coins in this condition may even have a little mint luster left.

VERY FINE (VF) Design still quite clear; however, the coin begins to show definite signs of wear. The lettering may be worn but the complete outline of every letter is still clear. The highest points of the design show smooth spots of wear.

FINE (F) A considerably worn but still desirable coin. The basic outline is still clear but much of the fine detail is lost. Portions of some of the lettering may be worn away.

VERY GOOD (VG) A much worn but not altogether unattractive coin. A coin in this condition should be free of serious gouges or other mutilations but it may be somewhat scratched from use.

GOOD (G) A really minimum condition coin. The date and mint mark would be legible and major portions of the design distinguishable.

FAIR Coins in fair condition are usually not acceptable to collectors. They may have only partial dates, be dark in color and parts of the design may be completely worn away. They are generally used as "space fillers" only until such time as a better coin can be had.

POOR Coins in poor condition are usually highly undesirable. They may be bent, corroded and completely worn down.

Now look at these coins (in their exact size) side by side and notice the variation.

In order to describe in detail just how these generalized terms apply to an actual coin, let's examine greatly enlarged photographs of the reverses of eight Liberty Head ("Barber") Quarters.

Note: Proofs are coins made especially for collectors at the mint. They are struck on polished planchets from polished dies which produce coins with brilliant mirror-like surfaces, sharp edges and perfect detail. Since they are not coins made in the normal manner and are never found in circulation, they are beyond the scope of this guide. In appearance, however, they have the same perfect detail as the uncirculated coins shown plus a mirror-like surface.

73

Uncirculated

All the details are sharply outlined:

the shield	the eagle's claws
the eagle's eye	the arrows
the eagle's neck	the leaves
the eagle's feathers	the dots in the border

the dots between "United" and "Quarter" and between "America" and "Dollar"
the lettering on the inscription
the lettering on the ribbon

Extremely Fine

All the details are still distinct.

Note, however, that there are slight scratches on the shield, and that the feathers are slightly faded toward the sides.

Very Fine

The eagle's eye and neck are distinct, and so are the arrows, the leaves, the dots and lettering on the inscription.

The shield is fairly distinct, but there are some nicks on it, and there are traces of fading toward the sides.

The feathers are considerably faded toward the sides, and the outside dots are beginning to grow fuzzy.

The claws are still fairly distinct, and so is the lettering on the ribbon, although *unum* is a little faded.

Fine

The shield and the eagle's eye are fairly distinct. However, there are some nicks and scratches on the shield and the fading toward the edges is getting more pronounced.

The neck is considerably faded, and the feathers are badly faded toward the sides.

The arrows, the leaves, and the lettering on the inscription are still distinct, and the dots in the inscription can be clearly seen.

The dots in the border have become fuzzier than in the previous condition.

The lettering on the ribbon is faded somewhat and several letters are unreadable.

The claws are no longer as distinct as they were previously.

(Note the "D" mint mark under the eagle.)

Very Good

The eagle's eye, the leaves, the dots and the lettering on the inscription are still distinct.

The lines on the shield are completely gone, and the details on the neck have almost disappeared.

Little of the detail on the feathers is left, and the claws seem to merge with the arrows and leaves.

The arrows have grown fuzzy, and the dots in the border are no longer distinct.

The lettering on the ribbon is badly faded and is becoming more unreadable.

Good

The shield is completely faded; all detail is gone on the neck.

The leaves, the inscription dots, and the inscription lettering are still distinct.

The eye is rather faint, the feathers are almost completely faded, and the claws are no longer sharply outlined.

The arrows are becoming fuzzy, and the dots in the border are considerably faded.

Most of the lettering on the ribbon is unreadable.

Fair

General comment: badly scratched and blotched.

The leaves are still distinct—the only good feature.

One of the inscription dots is clear, the other faded.

The inscription lettering is decidedly weaker than previously; the ribbon lettering is completely unreadable.

The claws are no longer sharply outlined, and the remaining features are completely rubbed off.

Poor

The leaves are still fairly distinct, but all the other details are completely or almost completely rubbed off.

6. WHAT COIN VALUES DEPEND ON

If you ask a non-collector his opinion of what makes a coin valuable, he will answer unhesitatingly, "Rarity!" It is true that rarity is a large part of the answer, but it is not the whole answer.

Again in the eyes of a non-collector, the age of a coin is also a prime factor in determining value. This is true to some extent, but again it is not the whole story. The coin trade has other standards besides age and rarity in assessing coin values.

Supply and demand

The number of collectors of United States coins has been growing steadily for years. The quantity of already-issued coins becomes smaller every year as coins disappear from circulation or into collections. The supply coming into the market from break-up of collections cannot keep pace with the demand that comes from ever greater numbers of collectors of American coins. Thus, the demand for these coins grows, while the supply diminishes. The result is a steadily rising level in the value of key American coins.

A collector still finds it fairly easy and at least relatively inexpensive to obtain the common coins of a type, but sooner or later he comes to want those coins of the series that are comparatively scarce. The only way to get them is to pay high premiums for them.

While collectors admire handsome coins and are fascinated by their historical associations, these factors likewise play a small part in measuring "demand" and in determining coin values. One of the most beautiful coins of all time is the one coined by Lysimachus of Thrace with the portrait of Alexander the Great. Famous as this much-admired coin is, its price in "very fine" condition is about $37.50. This is less than the price of many an American coin which is available in much larger quantities in very fine condition.

Condition

As we have seen in Chapter 5, there is considerable variation in the physical state of coins—their condition. Collectors set great store by condition. They like to obtain a coin in the finest possible state they can afford.

Because this attitude is universal among collectors, condition plays a very important part in determining the premium value of a coin. The 1892 dime (from the Philadelphia mint) is a typical example, as the following values indicate:

Good	$1.00	Extremely Fine	6.50
Fine	3.00	Uncirculated	25.00
Very Fine	4.00		

Mintage

Where there is a great variation in the number of coins issued, it is very likely that there will be a sizable difference in price.

The serious collector therefore finds it useful to be familiar with the quantities issued year by year, as shown in the annual mint reports.

The mint reports are in most cases a useful guide to values, but not in all cases. The early mint reports are sometimes unreliable; in such instances the extra coins may have been melted down or actually carry dates of the year before they were recorded.

Low mintage alone, however, is not enough to make a coin valuable. A coin may be scarce, but if there is little or no demand for it, then it will not be valuable. Lack of demand leaves prices on a fairly even keel. Many foreign and certainly most of the ancient coins are rare and the supply is limited, to be sure. But the demand for them is nothing like the demand for American coins which is why we have American coins that sell for several times the price of actually scarcer foreign and ancient coins.

This brings us to the purchase of coins for investment. How can we tell which coins are going to grow in demand in the years to come? Is there a way to predict such an intangible factor as demand? Tastes do change but there are several well-founded principles which will help you become a successful investor.

7. COINS FOR INVESTMENT

From the investment point of view, American coins are much more desirable than foreign coins. The values of United States coins have been rising steadily for a good many years. As far as we can foresee at the present time, this trend will continue. The supply of coins is limited, while the number of collectors increases steadily.

With demand increasing from year to year, a collector has a reasonable—though not infallible—assurance that the United States coins he buys will rise substantially in value in the years to come.

Uncirculated rolls

Most coin investors buy rolls of recent date uncirculated coins and put them away in anticipation of appreciation in value. Putting away uncirculated rolls provides a real feeling of "being in the market." A roll of cents is 50 shares of its issue with a recognized value on the coin market. It has a par value (face value) and a market value (its selling price to other investors). The number of pieces of each issue minted (the supply) is known. As with other commodities, the market value fluctuates with the popularity of (demand for) the issue.

Uncirculated rolls (or bags for big investors) are an exceptionally safe investment if you can obtain them at face value or just a small

Denomination	No. of coins per roll	Face value per roll	No. of rolls per bag	Face value per bag
CENTS	50	$ .50	100	$ 50.00
NICKELS	40	2.00	100	200.00
DIMES	50	5.00	100	500.00
QUARTERS	40	10.00	100	1,000.00
HALVES	20	10.00	100	1,000.00

Face value and number of pieces per standard roll and bag lots of U.S. coins.

premium above. If an issue does not go up in value as you expect, at least the face value of the coins is always assured. Unlike other kinds of investments, coins never become completely valueless.

If you can't get coins at face value, then buying by the roll at least entitles you to wholesale prices—a dealer can sell 50 coins in a roll at a much lower mark-up per unit than he must have when he sells coins one at a time. The spread between the buying and selling prices of uncirculated rolls is less than for any other kind of numismatic material. Current buy-sell listings in dealers' advertisements reveal an overall average mark-up of approximately 25%. This is in contrast to mark-ups of up to 50% and more on single coins. The mark-up on rolls of cents and nickels is less than it is on comparably scarce rolls of dimes, quarters and halves. Dealers offer to pay a much higher percentage of the market price to buy rolls that are in current demand. In checking the current buy-sell listings, some instances were noted where the buy-sell spread was as low as 12% on certain "hot" rolls.

Another advantage of investing in uncirculated rolls is that there are ready buyers and sellers for this material. It's easy to get up-to-date price information too, as every issue of the coin newspapers and magazines carries buy-sell ads for uncirculated rolls. Also, when it comes time to cash in your holdings, there are no disputes over condition as sometimes occur with used coins.

Which coins are most likely to increase in value?

To make a significant profit from coin investments, your money must go into the right issues. You can choose the best investments by studying *averages* and *percentages*. Here are some important facts for would-be investors: the average annual mintage per issue of each denomination during the 10-year period, 1953-1962:

cents	668,828,182
nickels	90,413,332
dimes	158,420,639
quarters	44,470,930
halves	15,137,534

85

If the number of coins minted for an issue falls substantially below the average for that denomination, you can take it as a sure indication of future appreciation. The three lowest mintage cents of this period, 1954, 1954-S and 1955-S were each less than 100,-000,000 and have already gone up considerably in price. Two later issues, the Philadelphia cents of 1957 (282,540,000 mintage) and 1958 (252,598,000 mintage) are nearly ⅔ less than the average mintage and are showing signs now of moving up in value. High mintage issues sometimes become valuable anyway, but coins with mintages substantially below the average are nearly always worthwhile investments.

1955 was a good year for investors as every denomination turned out to have something special. The 1955-S cent was the last coin of this denomination struck at the San Francisco mint and the lowest mintage cent since 1939. The 1955 nickel was also a low coinage for its series and, except for the 1950-D, it was also the lowest mintage since 1939. The 1955 dime is the lowest mintage coin of the entire Roosevelt series and we have to go back to 1938 to find a lower mintage among the Mercury dimes. The 1955-D quarter was the lowest mintage since 1940 and the 1955 half dollar was the second lowest mintage of the Franklin series. Here are some interesting statistics on these five coins:

		mintage	lowest advertised price per roll in 1955	advertised price in mid-1963	percentage increase
1955-S	1¢	44,610,000	1.00	40.00	3900%
1955	5¢	8,266,200	4.00	60.00	1400%
1955	10¢	12,828,381	6.00	45.00	683%
1955-D	25¢	13,959,000	11.00	60.00	445%
1955	50¢	2,876,381	11.00	24.00	118%

As you can see, the half dollar with by far the lowest actual mintage, increased the least in value percentagewise. The Lincoln cent with by far the greatest mintage increased the most in value. The answer to this seeming contradiction is that the interest in collecting Lincoln cents is proportionally that much greater than the interest in collecting Franklin halves.

Future demand is the key factor

The number of pieces originally minted has a bearing on future value, but the popularity of a series is even more important. Cent and nickel rolls are in much greater demand than rolls of dimes, quarters and halves. Always bear in mind that the demand for rolls of coins depends ultimately upon a demand for the individual coins. New collectors taking up the hobby favor cents and nickels because the face value is low and these denominations are plentiful in pocket change for checking.

The 1955 coins that we looked at were especially good investments. Does the same hold true for less spectacular coins? The chart on page 88 shows the price at which each issue was being advertised five years after its date of issue. Based on this table, the average percentage increase per roll for all U.S. coins issued during the period, 1950-1955, put away at face value and held for five years is:

cents	594%
nickels	344%
dimes	249%
quarters	61%
halves	69%

As these figures show again, an investor's chances for success are much greater with the lower denomination coins. After allowing for the spread between buying and selling prices, every issue of cents returned a profit, in some cases a sizable one. Nearly every nickel and dime roll provided some return but many quarters and halves were still worth little more than face value.

How soon do coins go up in value?

Unless an issue becomes "hot" (receives extraordinary publicity or for some reason is in great demand from the very beginning), significant price increases do not occur for the first two to three years. It takes that long for the roll dealers' initial stocks to be exhausted, when they must come into the market to replenish their stock at premium prices. It is only at that point that demand catches

Advertised selling prices and percentage of increase for uncirculated rolls of U.S. coins five years after their date of issue.

	CENTS Price	% Incr.	NICKELS Price	% Incr.	DIMES Price	% Incr.	QUARTERS Price	% Incr.	HALF DOLLARS Price	% Incr.
1950	$ 2.50	400%	$10.00	400%	$25.00	400%	$16.00	60%	$22.50	125%
1950-D	2.25	350	9.50	375	12.50	150	13.00	30	27.50	175
1950-S	2.50	400	Not Minted		75.00	1400	20.00	100	Not Minted	
1951	1.50	200	5.00	150	10.00	100	13.00	30	17.50	75
1951-D	1.25	150	6.50	225	9.00	80	12.50	25	17.50	75
1951-S	3.50	600	25.00	1150	65.00	1200	25.00	150	22.50	125
1952	2.00	300	3.00	50	8.00	60	12.50	25	13.00	30
1952-D	1.25	150	6.00	200	7.50	50	12.50	25	12.50	25
1952-S	4.00	700	3.00	50	25.00	400	20.00	100	15.00	50
1953	1.50	200	3.50	75	7.00	40	12.00	20	25.00	150
1953-D	1.50	200	4.00	100	6.50	30	12.00	20	12.50	25
1953-S	4.50	800	4.50	125	7.50	50	12.50	25	13.00	30
1954	10.00	1900	5.00	150	7.00	40	12.50	25	12.50	25
1954-D	3.00	500	4.00	100	6.50	30	13.00	30	12.50	25
1954-S	5.00	900	6.00	200	7.50	50	13.00	30	15.00	50
1955	6.50	1200	45.00	2150	35.00	600	25.00	150	25.00	150
1955-D	6.00	1100	12.00	500	32.50	550	37.50	275	Not Minted	
1955-S	10.00	1900	Not Minted		22.50	350	Not Minted		Not Minted	
1956	2.75	450	5.75	188	8.00	60	13.50	35	15.00	50
1956-D	2.25	350	5.75	188	8.00	60	17.50	75	Not Minted	
1957	2.75	450	5.75	188	7.50	50	13.50	35	15.00	50
1957-D	1.75	250	5.00	150	7.50	50	13.50	35	13.00	30
1958	3.50	600	18.00	800	12.00	140	17.00	70	16.00	60
1958-D	1.50	200	3.25	63	7.00	40	14.00	40	15.00	50

Average percentage increase for 1950-1958 rolls of uncirculated coins bought at face value and held for five years.

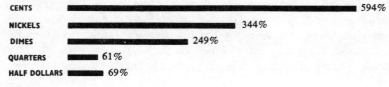

CENTS — 594%
NICKELS — 344%
DIMES — 249%
QUARTERS — 61%
HALF DOLLARS — 69%

up to the supply and prices start to move up. Prices then usually move up gradually but steadily for a few years until they reach a level where investors no longer consider the issue reasonably priced. At that point, the issue may coast along for some time with little change in price. By the time an issue is 8 to 10 years old, its relative rarity in relation to the other coins in its series is established and price increases from then on are in proportion to the over-all trend in the coin market.

If you are willing to venture a small premium on the coins you put away, it is often more profitable not to tie your money up in an issue the year it comes out. The performance of the 1957 Philadelphia cent illustrates this point. The advertised selling price per roll in 1957 was about 75¢. By 1959 it had reached $1.00, in 1961 the price was up to $2.50 and in 1963, it is advertised at $4.50.

If an investor bought rolls in 1957 and sold them after four years at $1.50 per roll, allowing for the buy-sell spread, his average annual return was 25%. Buying these same rolls in 1959 at $1.00 and selling four years later at $3.50 per roll returns an average annual profit of 62%. Unless you are able to get coins from banks at face value, you will find it more profitable not to buy them at premium prices until it appears that the issue is starting to move up in price.

There are investment possibilities in rolls that have already gone up in value. There is no question that the low mintage coins like 1954, 1954-S and 1955-S selling respectively in 1963 at about $25, $20 and $30 per roll will continue to go up in value. There is a point, however, when coins are priced above what the majority of collectors and investors will pay and the *percentage* of increase slows down. It sounds very good to buy a roll of cents at $20 and sell them two years later at $30. This $10 gain percentagewise is an annual return of 25%, but the same money put into rolls of cents at $1.00 each that can be sold in two years at $2.00 will return an annual 50% on your investment. Unless the coin is especially in demand it is much easier to find buyers at $2.00 per roll than at $30.

Going back to the special 1955 coins, the chart on p. 90 plots the yearly increase in value. On the chart, you will see that the 1955-S cent climbed steadily in value from the time it first appeared.

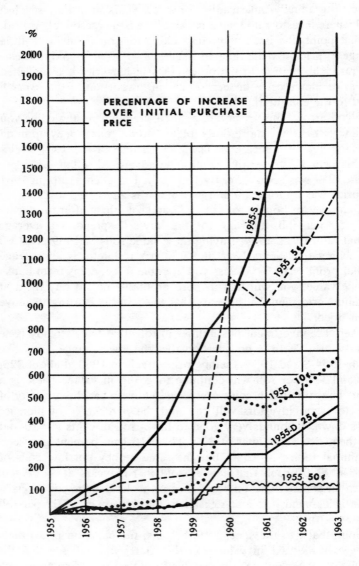

PERCENTAGE OF INCREASE OVER INITIAL PURCHASE PRICE

1955-S 1¢
1955 5¢
1955 10¢
1955-D 25¢
1955 50¢

It was widely publicized as the last "S" cent and the demand was so great that it brought a high premium even when there were still ample dealer stocks. The 1955 dime behaved in a more ordinary manner even though it was a very low mintage. This coin went up slowly until 1959 when dealers' initial stocks began to run out. It then climbed quickly to about $25 per roll, a reasonable price for a coin with such a low mintage and held at about that level for two years. It's true scarcity in relation to the rest of the series has finally been recognized and it is now moving up again, but an investor could have sold his holdings in 1960 for just as much as in 1962 and in the meantime invested his capital in another issue.

Timing

One investment theory holds that coins should be purchased at their lowest price—as they are issued. Then the coins should be held for a time (say ten years) in order to profit from the ensuing appreciation in the value of the coins.

While this method is good in theory, it must be applied in a flexible manner. Some coins will go up rapidly in value; others will move sluggishly. Some coins may even fluctuate in value from year to year, or they may level off temporarily. Thus, timing of buying and selling turns out to be of the utmost importance, and keen judgment of market trends is required.

As was pointed out above, timing is all important in buying and selling. After constant price rises there are breathing spells when prices level off; then, later on, the upward trend is resumed. The collector who studies the movements of coin prices will be careful to buy when prices have temporarily leveled off, and avoid selling during those periods.

When prices are going up steadily, the problem is much more complicated. It takes very good judgment and plenty of experience on the collector's part to determine whether a price rise has reached its peak for the time being, or whether the upward movement is to continue. Thus, buying and selling decisions become extremely complex.

Any collector who contemplates investing in coins should realize before he starts that he will have to deal with a great many complex variables: the amounts he will have available for investment; the length of time he can sit back and wait for a substantial profit; the general trend of financial, economic and business conditions; the profit that might be realized from alternative investments; changes in fashion among coin collectors; the possibility that certain coins might be subject to speculative manipulation.

Used coins as investments

It is possible to find coins in circulation that are worthwhile putting away for future appreciation. If you count the value of the time involved in finding them, however, it is not an attractive prospect if your sole purpose is profit. On the other hand, if you are building up a collection and are checking coins in circulation anyway, then it is certainly worthwhile to put aside those pieces with good chances of growing in value.

A collector still finds it fairly easy and at least relatively inexpensive to obtain the common coins of a type, but sooner or later he comes to want those coins of the series that are comparatively scarce. The only way to get them is to pay high premiums for them. These coins, then, are the ones that are always in demand to fill those "nearly-completed" sets. As you would expect, analysis of price trends shows that key coins are not only much higher in price than the common coins of a series, but they also are the ones which show the most rapid increases in price. In fact, these "controller" coins set the pace for the whole coin market.

Here is a useful list of the chief controller coins which have promising investment possibilities:

Indian Head Cents: 1864 (L on Ribbon); 1869; 1870; 1871; 1872; 1877; 1908S; 1909S. In general, the issues of the 1870's are the scarcest in this series.

Lincoln Head Cents: 1909S (VDB); 1909S; 1910S; 1911S; 1912S; 1913S; 1914D; 1914S; 1915S; 1921S; 1922D; 1923S; 1924D; 1924S; 1926S; 1931D; 1931S; 1933; 1933D; 1939D; 1954; 1955S.

Buffalo Nickels: Almost all the D and S coins through 1928 have already risen so steeply as to be beyond the reach of the average collector, unless he is content with the inferior conditions.

Jefferson Nickels: 1938D; 1938S; 1939D; 1939S; 1942D; 1949S; 1950; 1950D; 1951S; 1955.

Mercury Head Dimes: 1916D; 1919D; 1919S; 1921P; 1921D; 1926S; 1927D; 1942D (over '41). Among short issues which look promising are 1930S; 1931D; 1931S.

Roosevelt Dimes: 1949S; 1950S; 1951S; 1955; 1955D,S.

Standing Liberty Quarters: 1916; 1917D,S (two varieties); 1918S (over '17); 1919D,S; 1923S; 1926S; 1927S. Comparatively short issues which are still reasonably priced include 1926D; 1927D; 1929D,S; 1930S.

Washington Quarters: 1932D; 1932S; 1936D; 1938; 1955D.

Standing Liberty Half Dollars: 1916; 1917D,S; 1919P,D,S; 1921P,D,S; 1938D. Most of these are so high in extremely fine or uncirculated condition as to price the ordinary collector out of the market.

Franklin Half Dollars: 1948; 1949; 1955.

Older coins as investments

Any Lincoln cent prior to 1935 is already worth double face value in fine condition or better. The mint mark pieces especially will go up in value since they are already disappearing from circulation and this is the first series of coins new collectors work on. Later dates are still readily available in uncirculated condition but as these become scarcer and more expensive a demand will grow for these same coins in used condition. Any of the dates from 1934 on with mintages below 50,000,000 pieces will be worth a premium in used condition within the next few years.

Buffalo nickels with clear dates are fast disappearing from daily change. Nearly every issue prior to 1929 is worth some premium if the date and mint mark are sharp. Jefferson nickels with mintages below 10,000,000 pieces are potentially valuable.

As with the uncirculated coins, the higher denominations do not go up in value as fast as cents and nickels. Many coins of these denominations already worth a premium turn up in circulation, but those dates that are still worth face value only are not likely to become more valuable very quickly. The only recent dates that are worth saving in used condition are those that are already expensive in uncirculated condition.

The trouble with older coins as investments is that they have already found their level between supply and demand on the numismatic market. All U.S. coins seem destined to go up in value as new collectors take up the hobby and more and more of the available coins disappear into albums. Generally, the higher the price a coin has reached, the less likelihood there is of high percentage profits, and the less return there is on the money invested. The older coins move along in relation to the over-all coin market. The investor is looking for situations where coins are advancing faster than the average. This does not mean that collectors shouldn't buy older coins. On the contrary, for pure interest, older coins are much more fascinating than new issues. The average collector is at least as much interested in the pleasure he gets from owning and keeping a coin as he is in the profit he will realize when he sells it. If bought at a fair price, nearly any coin is a good investment for a collector since he will enjoy it while he has it.

Successful investing

The safest coin investments are uncirculated rolls bought at or near face value. The greatest potential for profit is in rolls of the lower denominations with mintages substantially less than average for the series. Little increase in value can be expected until an issue is two or three years old. At that point, coins begin to seek their proper level in the coin market based on the availability and popularity of the issue and series. Unless an unusual demand develops, investors putting new coins away during the year of issue must expect to hold them for at least 5 to 6 years before they see a rewarding increase in value. Investors willing to pay a small premium for coins do best to watch for issues already a few years old and just beginning to move up in value. Unless you are really knowledgeable about the coin market, it is risky to invest in rolls that have already appreciated to high levels. The successful investor strives for a high percentage of increase on his capital.

8. HOW COINS ARE MADE

Nowadays the making of coins has been mechanized to an uncanny degree of efficiency. To begin with, all coins of a given type have a standardized content. For example, every penny contains 950 parts copper to 50 parts zinc. In the case of silver coins, 900 parts silver are alloyed with 100 parts copper. The metals are weighed in huge quantities on a remarkably sensitive balance that is accurate to one-hundredth of an ounce.

After weighing, the metals pass to an electric furnace, where they are melted. The alloy is prepared in a liquid state and formed into thin bars in molds. Two checking processes verify the proportions in the alloyed metal.

The bars are then passed through several rollers to be softened and stretched into thin strips. The bars used for pennies end up as strips eight feet long and 48/1000th of an inch thin.

Ingenious punch machines hammer 500 blank coins out of each strip, four at a time. The wasted metal is gathered and melted down for future use. When the punching process is over the blanks are too hard for immediate use, and they are softened by means of an annealing process. But this introduces a new complication, as it stains the blanks; so they are passed to machines which wash and dry them.

The blanks are now ready for the milling machine, which thickens the edges to make the coins last longer. At last they are ready to have designs stamped on them by automatic, high-speed machines in the Press Room. A pressure of 40 tons is enough for stamping pennies, whereas silver dollars (which have not been coined since 1935) required a pressure of 160 tons. Such a press produces 10,000 finished coins in a single hour.

Each coin is impressed between a pair of dies, an obverse ("heads," normally the top die) and a reverse ("tails," normally on the bottom). A "collar" attached to the bottom die holds the planchet in place and keeps it from spreading out as the dies come together. Blank planchets are fed into the press and finished coins are ejected in an automatic, continuous flow. A die is only serviceable for a limited number of impressions before it must be replaced. Repeated impressions wear away the fine detail of the die and the resulting coins are no longer "sharp."

Making the dies

For the design to stand up in relief on the finished coin, it must be cut (incused) into the die. Occasionally, a die will crack or chip while still in use. When this happens the crack impresses itself onto the coins as a line, an unintentional addition to the design. A chip in the die appears as a dot on the coin. Working the other way, waste material can clog up part of a die. When part of the die is filled in, that portion of the design (usually a letter or numeral) is not impressed on the coin.

(Left) Reverse of the 1795 silver dollar with two leaves below the eagle's wing and (right) with three leaves. The slight variation shows that they were struck from different dies even though both are dated 1795.

All details of the dies from which the earliest American coins were struck were engraved directly onto steel by the hands of skilled workmen. The steel was then hardened, making a die. Variations in the design of coins from these different dies are not difficult to see. One 1795 half dime shows the head of Liberty with six locks of hair while coins from other dies show her with seven. Similarly, on 1795 silver dollars there are varieties with two leaves on the branch below the eagle's wing, others with three leaves. A feature or a combination of features that make it possible to differentiate between coins struck from one pair of dies as opposed to coins from all other dies of that date is said to be "diagnostic of the die."

In about 1795, with the introduction of the draped bust of Liberty design on our coins, punches or hubs were used for the major parts of the design like the heads and the eagles, and there was no longer

(Left) Wide-date, and (right) narrow-date cent of 1817. During this period, the stars and digits of the date were stamped individually into the dies. Note also that the left coin has 13 stars, the right one 15 stars.

any variation in the design of these features. Letters, numerals and stars were still punched in one at a time and it's possible to distinguish between these dies by comparing the relative size and position of these portions of the design.

When the Seated Liberty design came into use about 1838, the complete design except the date and mint mark was put into each working die from the same master hub. Modern coins are struck from dies prepared from a master hub that even includes the date. If the impression is not satisfactory, the workman may give the die another blow with the master punch or individual letters can be recut by hand. The mint marks are still punched in separately, causing minor variations in the relative position of the letter.

Errors can occur at several steps in the coining process and varieties can be created in preparing the dies. The following chapter tells about the most interesting kinds of oddities and provides an explanation of how they come about.

9. VARIETIES, ODDITIES AND ERRORS

Strange terms like "bugs-bunny" half dollars, "adam's apple" quarters, "fanged" Roosevelt dimes, double-profile nickels, "cracked-skull" and "dagger-in-back" Lincoln cents have found their way into numismatics lately.

Oddity collectors tend to give their discoveries fanciful names. This "cracked skull" cent is so named because of the prominent die breaks across Lincoln's head.

Until a few years ago, collectors looked for the "plain," "D," and "S" mint issues of each coin and except for obvious overdates and changes of design, that was it. Now, however, collectors examine coins with magnifying glasses, even microscopes, searching for new varieties. The fanciful names for some of the discoveries have caused some of the old-time collectors to wonder whether these "flyspeck" collectors aren't ruining the hobby, but just the opposite is true. The enthusiasm over varieties has put a new challenge into collecting.

Varieties, oddities and errors give collectors something more to look for. Now that only two mints are striking coins, with little likelihood that any more special commemoratives will be authorized, new issues alone are not enough to sustain interest in a collection. And as date and mint mark sets approach completion, it can be a long time between "finds" unless you look for varieties too.

Interest in varieties causes collectors to study their coins, to inquire about how they are made and how varieties and errors come about. You are sure to hear more soon about varieties, as they are added to catalogue listings and given spaces in albums. They are worth knowing about, since a growing demand for this kind of material will definitely result in significant price increases.

How they happen

Here are the kinds of errors and how they happen.

This blank nickel planchet slipped past the dies without having the design impressed. Note, however, that it did go through a milling machine which thickened or "upset" the edge.

BLANK PLANCHET—The coin-shaped piece of metal, called the planchet or flan, sometimes passes through the minting process without being impressed between the dies.

CLIPPED PLANCHET—The planchets are punched out of a strip of metal passing through a cutting machine. Imperfect planchets with a circular "bite" are the result of successive punches made too close together. A "straight-edge" planchet would come from a punch too close to the end of the strip. These cutting errors are fairly common and since they can easily be simulated outside the mint they have little premium value.

OFF-CENTER COIN—If the planchet is not properly centered between the dies, only a portion of the design appears on the coin. Sometimes the planchet is nearly blank with just a small part of the design showing.

DOUBLE-STRUCK COIN—If the coin is not ejected properly after being struck, a second impression is made on the same planchet. The second impression is frequently off center as well.

This picture shows a bronze planchet intended for a Lincoln cent that has been impressed with the Jefferson nickel design. The lettering runs off the edge of the coin since the copper planchet is smaller than the nickel dies.

OFF-METAL COIN—These occur when a planchet intended for a coin in one metal is inadvertently mixed with planchets of another metal. Silver cents struck on dime planchets are the variety most often found. Under the present laws, it is illegal to hold this kind of error. Technically, no coin is legal until it is authorized and issued for circulation. Even then it is illegal unless it corresponds in all respects to the authorization. Cents, of course, are not authorized in silver.

Inadvertent mixing of planchets also explains wrong-size coins, such as a quarter struck on a dime planchet. Off-metal coins are scarce and would probably be worth $50-$100 if they could be legally traded.

OVERSIZE COIN—A thinner, oversize "pancake" coin with rounded edges occurs when the collar does not contain the coin properly.

A cracked die reveals itself as a raised line on the coins struck from it. This nickel (enlarged) shows a die break line extending across all four legs of the buffalo. Nickel is the least malleable of the coinage metals and is very hard on dies.

DIE BREAK—A break or crack in the working die causes a similar raised mark on the surface of the coin (connected letters, etc.).

FILLED DIE—If part of a die fills up with metal scraps or other material, that portion does not impress itself on the coins resulting in missing letters, numbers, etc.

BROCKAGE—A coin showing the same design on both sides; one perfectly struck, the other an incuse mirror image. Caused by the preceding coin sticking to one of the dies.

LAMINATED PLANCHET—If the planchet metal is not properly annealed (softened and made less brittle), pieces of metal strip off or peel away.

DOUBLE DIE, DOUBLE PROFILE, DOUBLE LETTERS or **DATE**—If the master die shifts or bounces between punches into a working die, all of the coins struck from that die will show a double impression of the design. A double strike can occur too if a coin sticks in the die and is impressed a second time. If it shifts the tiniest fraction between impressions, at least part of the design will be doubled. One impression is almost a "shadow" of the other. All of a coin's design does not appear doubled in these situations; the second strike wipes out or hides the first strike on some parts of the coin.

DOUBLE MINT MARK—Mint letters are struck by hand into the die before it goes out to the branch mint. If the workman shifts his punch at all between blows, the die will have a doubly-impressed mint letter. Coins struck with such a die will show a double mint mark.

OVERDATE—Infrequently, through error or emergency need for coins, older dies have been stamped over with the current date. The earlier numeral shows up below the new one (such as a 2 on top of a 1 which looks a little like a dollar sign).

OVERSTRUCK MINT MARK—This is a situation similar to an overdate. If a workman strikes a coin first with the wrong punch and then corrects his error, a trace of the first letter may appear. When there was more than one branch mint, the mint letter on a die prepared for one could be restamped and sent to a different branch.

RECUT DATE OR LETTER—Worn dies can be reconditioned for sharper impressions by recutting worn letters or numerals. The recut portion shows a faint outline.

A recent widely publicized die variation is in the 1960 cent. (Left) Large-date variety. The top of the "9" extends above "1," "6" has a long tail and the "0" is decidedly round. (Right) Small-date variety.

LARGE AND SMALL DATES, MICROSCOPIC MINT MARKS, etc.—These varieties are relative to each other. They occur when two sets of punches of different sizes are used in preparing dies or when there is a change in the master die during the course of the year.

10. COLLECTING U.S. COINS

When you start collecting coins, your interest is usually drawn first to the coins of your own country. Sometimes you find or are given an old coin of a type that has been out of use for many years and, in looking for information about that one coin, you find yourself caught up in the fascinating study of coins. More often, however, your interest is attracted to the kinds of coins to be found right in your pocket, you read articles in the newspapers or hear stories that coins of great value are being found in circulation or that errors in coinage have inadvertently been released by the mint.

Regardless of how you have been attracted to coin collecting, your first experience with the hobby will very likely be the formation of a "date and mint mark collection" from the coins still to be found in circulation.

What to collect?

The first decision you must make is which series or denominations of the available coins, from cents to silver dollars, you are going to begin collecting. Many beginners choose to start with the Lincoln cents. It is an ideal choice because the face value of a complete set is only about $1.50, whereas that of a silver dollar collection is well over $100.00. Since you will probably find yourself with a pocketful of pennies at the end of most days, it will be easy to find coins to look through for dates that you need. The design of the Lincoln

The two most popular series for beginners are Lincoln cents (left) and Jefferson nickels (right). New collectors usually start with the lower denomination coins and work up to the higher.

cent has been the same for over 50 years and the dates are one of the last features of the design to wear away, so it is still possible to find many of the older issues in circulation. The relative quantities of common dates and scarce dates in this series are in about the right proportion for you to be able to get off to a flying start, finding many different coins right away, yet completing the collection is difficult enough to present a real challenge.

It is still possible to complete a set of Roosevelt dimes (right) from coins found in circulation. Mercury dimes (left) can also be found, but many of the earlier dates are scarce.

There is no reason, of course, why you cannot collect more than one denomination at the same time. A good plan, however, is to concentrate on one series first, such as the Lincoln cents. If an older date nickel or dime comes along, hold on to it for later but at the moment give your main attention to one series. For the first weeks of your collecting, you will probably discover at least one coin a day.

Standing Liberty (left) and Washington quarters (right) can be found in change but the dates of many of the earlier coins have been completely worn off, making them valueless to collectors.

As your collection fills out, however, it will become more difficult to find dates that you need and things will slow down a bit. When this happens, switch your attention to the next collection, such as Jefferson nickels. You should continue to watch for the cents needed to complete that set but your main activity and effort should be with the new series. Follow the same procedure to keep your interest from lagging by moving on to the next series when this collection slows down.

Coins from circulation

In forming a collection of coins from circulation, there are two things that you must try to do. The first is to find one coin of each different date, from each different mint. One specimen of each issue constitutes a full set of any given series. Your second goal must be to find the coins in the best possible condition. Superior-condition coins are certainly more pleasing to own and display. The finer they are, the more desirable, and hence more valuable, they are likely to become in the future.

The large size of Walking Liberty (top) and Franklin half dollars (below) makes them attractive in collections. There are some scarce dates in both series but it is possible to find all of them in circulation.

The first and most obvious place to look for coins is right in your pocket. The majority of new collectors start out with "date and mint mark" collections of the current American coins, usually of the lower denominations—Lincoln cents, Jefferson nickels and Roosevelt dimes. All of these collections are appropriate for beginners, since quite a few of the coins can be found right away. On the other hand, there are a few scarce issues in each set which make them just difficult enough to give the budding collector a sense of accomplishment when his set is completed.

When you are ready to start on your collection, the very first thing is to begin checking the coins that pass through your hands each day. To do this efficiently, be sure to have a separate pocket or purse where you can put each coin given you during the day. Check your pocket coins as soon as possible against your collection and any coins not wanted can be put back in your regular change pocket to be given out again the next day. The secret of finding coins with scarce dates in circulation is to be consistent. If you are watching your coins, watch all of them. If you only look at the date when you "think it might be a good one," you are bound to let most of the scarcer ones slip right by.

When you are ready to check coins against your collection, sit down near a strong light. Pick up one of the coins to be checked and read the date and mint mark. Turn to the space provided in your album for that particular coin. If the space is empty, you have made a "find" and you place the coin in it. If the space is filled, compare the condition of the new coin with the one already there and retain the better of the two pieces.

You may wish to search through more coins than come your way in daily change. It is possible to purchase rolls of coins from banks and you may also be able to arrange to go through coins taken in at neighborhood stores, from parking meters, vending machines, collection plates, etc. If you are searching through large quantities of coins, you will find it helpful to make or buy a set of forms to facilitate sorting.

A few duplicates of each issue can be saved for trading stock although it is pointless to save too many of any one issue. For instance, if you are able to find 25 or 50 pieces of the same item, you can be sure that any potential trader you meet will have found at least the one specimen of that issue needed for his own set.

If you do save duplicates, remember always to save the ones in best condition. Some collectors like to work on a "second set" of each series which they keep exclusively for "trade bait." If you are fortunate enough to find extras of any of the really scarce dates, you can easily sell them to a coin dealer at a good price.

Buying coins

In every series of coins there are a few dates, called "key coins" or "controller coins," that are very difficult to find in circulation. In order to increase or complete your set you may want to buy some of the coins needed. Remember that the rarer and more in demand a coin is, the more expensive it is likely to be.

Nearly every city of any size has at least one professional coin dealer. Leading department stores across the country have special sections devoted exclusively to the needs of coin collectors. An extensive mail order business is conducted in the coin field so even those living in remote areas can be served. Coin dealers can be of assistance to you in many ways other than just selling you coins and supplies although this is certainly their main function. Department store coin departments and coin stores usually have extensive displays that are most instructive to the new collector. You can learn a great deal about coins, collections and display methods by studying the way coins are shown in a store. You can see nearly all of the different kinds of coins—American, foreign and ancient— in one place and test your own interests. Coin dealers vie to outdo each other in having the latest books, albums and other innovations to make the hobby easier and more pleasant for the collector.

Most coin dealers have had considerable experience with coins, collecting and collectors, and are often able to give you helpful and sound advice about your own projects and plans. A collector usually establishes a relationship with a favorite dealer on whom he can depend for special attention, suggestions and reliable merchandise.

Building your collection

After you have done all you can about finding coins in circulation, when your sets are as nearly complete as you can make them, you have to plan to buy any additional coins you want.

You may decide to carry your sets of current series a step further in upgrading them by purchasing coins in new, uncirculated condition.

Seeking better specimens and "upgrading" the coins already in your collection gives you just that much more opportunity to work with your coins. The challenge is greater and so is the sense of achievement when the collection finally measures up to the highest standards.

Once a coin comes into your possession, even if it is a badly worn specimen, you should be careful to see that no further damage is done to it. Coins should always be picked up and held by the edges. Copper coins, uncirculated and proof coins of all types are particularly susceptible to damage by "fingering," but it is advisable to get into the habit of handling all coins carefully. Needless to say, you should be careful about letting coins drop. A fall of just a few inches onto a hard surface can put an ugly dent on the edge of a prize coin. Many collectors make a practice of holding their coins above a pad or cloth when examining them.

Coins should never be kept loose in bags or boxes. Larger coins such as half dollars that have sizable areas of smooth surface and reeded edges scratch each other up very badly. Again, it is a good idea to keep all coins in such a manner that they do not come into contact with one another.

Cleaning coins

Collectors disagree on the advisability of cleaning coins, but the general feeling is that it is best to refrain or at least to proceed with a great deal of caution. The purpose of any cleaning should be to restore a coin as nearly as possible to its original appearance. There is nothing quite so distressing to the knowledgeable collector as a nice coin that has been spoiled by being rubbed with an eraser, scrubbed with a wire brush, buffed to a high gloss or otherwise "improved."

All silver coins, particularly the uncirculated pieces, tarnish in time—regardless of how carefully you protect them. If you feel you must clean uncirculated coins, use some kind of liquid cleaner, not one of the abrasive pastes. For used silver coins, a paste of baking soda and water will effectively remove the film of dirt and grime acquired in circulation and even the dirtiest coins can be made to look presentable. Beware, however, of too much rubbing or the coins will be unattractively shiny and too obviously cleaned. Many collectors prefer nicely toned coins to those that are bright. The silver coins particularly take on an attractive "blue tone" with age.

On your copper coins, use a little olive oil on a soft cloth to remove most of the scum picked up in circulation. Nothing much can be done about changing the color of a used copper coin. If you plan any experiments of your own along these lines, be sure to practice on coins that are not of value to your collection.

A final caution is that you may unwittingly reduce the value of a coin by cleaning it. If you do not care about disposing of your coins, then by all means go ahead and clean them if you wish. There are those collectors, however, who prefer uncleaned coins and are not at all interested in specimens that have been shined up. On the other hand, those who do like bright coins may have their own favorite methods of cleaning them. You may find it more difficult to dispose of coins that have been cleaned than those that are left "as is."

Specialized collecting

Eventually, almost every collector finds that one phase of collecting has a particular appeal for him and decides to form a specialized collection dealing with his favorite subject. In this area there are no definite rules to follow and the numismatist (the collector who has become a student of coins is now worthy of the title) must be guided by his own interest and ability. He may pursue a specialty in conjunction with the more usual date and mint mark or type collections or he may wish to devote all of his attention to his pet project. Through years of interest in numismatics, it is not unusual for a collector to concentrate at different times on various phases of the hobby.

Shield (left), Liberty Head (center) and Buffalo nickels (two on right) can all be collected by date but there are rare dates in each set. For example, there were only about 500 pieces struck dated 1877.

110

You can extend your date and mint mark method of collecting to the obsolete series such as Indian cents, and Liberty Head nickels, dimes, quarters and halves.

Date and mint mark collections of Seated Liberty (left) and Barber (right) dimes can be assembled. There are scarce dates in each set, but m‌‌ of these coins are available from dealers for a small premi‌‌.

Your interest may be drawn to early American coins, and you can study and form a type collection representing the various issues.

Date and mint mark collections can be extended to include the Seated Liberty (left) and Barber (right) quarters.

You may decide to make a specialized collection of one particular series of coins.

Many of the early date half dollars were struck in relatively large numbers and can be purchased very reasonably in relation to their age.

You may find it more appealing to specialize in one of the unusual types of money that have been used at various times in our history.

Collecting by type

Gathering a "type set" of American coins is a form of collecting greatly favored by collectors. In fact, it is the second most popular way to collect United States coins. In a type collection, one coin serves to represent all the different issues of the same design or style, i.e., of the same "type."

Thus the collection would contain one Indian Head cent, of any date, to represent all of the bronze Indian Head cents issued from 1864 through 1909. Two Liberty Head nickels would be shown; a specimen of the type struck only in 1883 without "CENTS" on the reverse, and another of any date from 1883 to 1912 representing all the issues of those years with "CENTS" on the reverse. Modern

Collectors regard the two designs of the 1883 Liberty nickel as different "types." The variety without "CENTS" was issued first, but unscrupulous people gold-plated them and passed them off as $5 gold pieces. To remedy the situation, the word "CENTS" was added to the later issues and continued to appear on subsequent dates.

coins would be treated similarly, a single specimen serving for series such as Washington quarters and Franklin halves that have appeared without variations since first introduced. Jefferson nickels would be represented by two coins; one for the normal issues, and one coin to exemplify the wartime, silver content pieces.

For the entire life of the coin from 1865 to 1889, the same design was used on all of the nickel 3¢ pieces.

An obsolete denomination such as the nickel three-cent piece would require only one coin as the design remained the same throughout its period of use, from 1865 to 1889. But the silver three-cent series would call for two pieces: one to represent the first issues of 1851 through 1853, and one for the later issues of 1854 through 1873. (An olive sprig was added to the reverse in 1854 indicating a change in the fineness of the silver being used, thereby creating a new type.)

An olive sprig and a bundle of arrows were added to the reverse of the silver 3¢ pieces in 1854, thus creating two "types" for collectors.

A type collector normally chooses one of the commoner dates of a series and purchases it for a fraction of the price of the rarities since it serves equally well to represent the type. Often, in the same series, the price of a poor-condition coin of a scarce date will be about the same as a choice-condition coin of a common date. For purposes of type collecting, it is usually preferable to acquire the best condition possible.

From 1793 to the present, counting all denominations from half cents to silver Trade Dollars, there have been about one hundred major types of American coins issued. Collectors are not in perfect agreement in all cases as to just how much of a change must occur to create a new type. For example, on the Seated Liberty coins of 1840 through 1891 there is a fold of drapery below the elbow that

There were two styles of 1839 Seated Liberty half dollars, with and without a fold of drapery at the elbow. This is considered a minor variation, not really a great enough difference to create separate "types."

did not appear on the figure of the Seated Liberty coins issued from 1838 through 1840. If you ask type collectors whether this is all one type or whether each should be counted as a separate type, you can get some pretty convincing arguments both ways.

Most coin catalogs indicate the various types of coins in their listings.

A great deal can be said in favor of collecting coins by type. You will get special satisfaction from displaying or showing a collection of this kind because every coin is different, and there is some history in back of each one. When collecting by type, you will own and learn the stories of many of our older, historically interesting coins, yet you can keep the cost at a level that is not prohibitive.

For example, in looking at a type collection, you can point to the two-cent piece which was the first American coin to bear the motto, "In God We Trust," brought about as a result of intensified religious sentiment during the Civil War. Most people are surprised to learn that the first coin struck in nickel was not a five-cent but a

The two-cent piece was the first coin to have the motto, "In God We Trust," which was added during a wave of religious sentiment at the height of the Civil War.

three-cent piece. You can turn, in a type collection, to the Trade Dollar, the only U.S. coin ever to have been recalled. A type collection embraces coins issued over a period of more than a century and a half and you will find it entertaining to read and think about the ideas and times they represent. A little background reading greatly enhances the enjoyment you can get from such a collection.

The Trade Dollar was the only U.S. coin ever recalled. Although it has slightly more silver in it than the standard dollar, it is not legal tender and thus has no "face value."

To get a general survey of the various types of U.S. coins, the following table will be useful.

Basic Design Types of United States Coins

Half Cent:
Liberty Cap Type

Half Cent:
Draped Bust Type

Half Cent:
Turban Head Type

HALF CENTS
    1793   Liberty Cap, head facing left
    1794–1797   Liberty Cap, head facing right
    1800–1808   Draped Bust
    1809–1836   Turban Head
    1849–1857   Braided Hair

Cent: Chain, 1793,
    reverse

Cent: Wreath, 1793.

Cent: Liberty Cap,
    1794

Draped Bust, 1797

Turban Head, 1810

115

LARGE CENTS

1793	Chain reverse
1793	Wreath reverse
1793–1796	Liberty Cap on pole
1796–1807	Draped Bust
1808–1814	Turban Head
1816–1839	Coronet
1839–1857	Braided Hair

The Flying Eagle Cent, showing an eagle in graceful flight, is one of the handsomest American coins.

SMALL CENTS

1856–1858	Flying Eagle
1859	Indian Head, no shield on reverse
1860–1864	Indian Head, shield, copper-nickel composition
1864–1909	Indian Head, shield, bronze
1909–1958	Lincoln Head, bronze
1943	Lincoln Head, steel
1959–	Lincoln Head, Memorial reverse

Two Cents Bronze

Three Cents Nickel

TWO CENTS
1864–1873 Shield obverse

THREE CENTS (NICKEL)
1865–1889 Liberty Head

THREE CENTS (SILVER)
1851–1853 Star
1854–1873 Star, olive branch and arrows on reverse

FIVE CENTS (NICKEL)
    1866–1867 Shield, rays on reverse
    1867–1883 Shield, no rays on reverse
    1883   Liberty Head, without "CENTS" on reverse
    1883–1912 Liberty Head, "CENTS" on reverse
    1913   Buffalo on mound
    1913–1938 Buffalo on straight line
    1938–   Jefferson Head
    1942–1945 Jefferson Head, silver content

Half Dime: Bust Type   Half Dime: Liberty Seated Type

HALF DIMES
    1794–1795 Flowing Hair
    1796–1797 Draped Bust, small eagle
    1800–1805 Draped Bust, large eagle
    1829–1837 Capped Bust
    1837–1838 Liberty Seated, no stars
    1838–1859 Liberty Seated, stars
    1853–1855 Liberty Seated, stars, arrows at date
    1860–1873 Liberty Seated, legend on obverse

Left: Dime, Bust Type (1828). *Right:* Dime, Liberty Seated Type (1837).

DIMES
    1796–1797 Draped Bust, small eagle
    1798–1807 Draped Bust, large eagle
    1809–1828 Capped Bust, large size
    1828–1837 Capped Bust, small size
    1837–1838 Liberty Seated, no stars
    1838–1860 Liberty Seated, stars

117

DIMES *continued*

1853–1855 Liberty Seated, stars, arrows at date
1860–1891 Liberty Seated, legend on obverse
1873–1874 Liberty Seated, legend, arrows at date
1892–1916 Liberty Head
1916–1945 Mercury Head
1946– Roosevelt Head

TWENTY CENTS

1875–1878 Liberty Seated

Left: Quarter, Bust Type. *Right:* Quarter, Liberty Seated Type.

QUARTERS

1796   Draped Bust, small eagle
1804–1807 Draped Bust, large eagle
1815–1828 Capped Bust, large size
1831–1838 Capped Bust, small size
1838–1865 Liberty Seated, no motto
1853   Liberty Seated, arrows at date, rays on reverse
1854–1855 Liberty Seated, arrows at date
1866–1891 Liberty Seated, motto on reverse
1873–1874 Liberty Seated, motto, arrows at date
1892–1916 Liberty Head
1916–1917 Liberty Standing, no stars below eagle
1917–1930 Liberty Standing, stars below eagle
1932–   Washington Head

Left: Half Dollar, Bust Type (1796). *Right:* Half Dollar, Liberty Seated Type (1840).

HALF DOLLARS

1794–1795	Flowing Hair
1796–1797	Draped Bust, small eagle
1801–1807	Draped Bust, large eagle
1807–1836	Capped Bust, lettered edge
1836–1837	Capped Bust, milled edge, "50 CENTS" on reverse
1838–1839	Capped Bust, milled edge, "HALF DOL" on reverse
1839–1866	Liberty Seated, no motto on reverse
1853	Liberty Seated, arrows at date, rays on reverse
1854–1855	Liberty Seated, arrows at date
1866–1891	Liberty Seated, motto on reverse
1873–1874	Liberty Seated, arrows at date
1892–1915	Liberty Head
1916–1947	Liberty Walking
1948–1963	Franklin Head
1964–	Kennedy Head

Left: Dollar, Bust Type (1796). *Right:* Dollar, Liberty Seated Type (1840).

SILVER DOLLARS

1794–1795	Flowing Hair
1795–1798	Draped Bust, small eagle
1798–1804	Draped Bust, large eagle

119

SILVER DOLLARS *continued*
    1840–1865 Liberty Seated, no motto
    1866–1873 Liberty Seated, motto
    1878–1921 Liberty Head
    1921–1935 Peace type

Trade Dollar (1873).
Left: obverse.
Right: reverse.

TRADE DOLLAR
    1873–1885 Liberty Seated

GOLD COINS

American gold coins were issued fairly regularly from 1795, the third year of operation at the U.S. mint, until the abandonment of the gold standard in 1933. Today, some Americans have never seen a gold coin, and for others gold coins are just fond memories. Of the many millions of dollars' worth of gold coins struck over the years, only a comparative handful are still in existence. Most of these repose in established coin collections and are among their owners' most prized possessions. Every serious collection should contain at least one gold coin as a representative of the important role gold has played in our coinage history.

GOLD DOLLARS:

Liberty Head
Type

Indian-Head-
dress Type

Larger Indian-
Headdress
Type

QUARTER EAGLES:

Liberty Cap   Liberty Head   Ribbon Type

Coronet Type   Indian Head Incuse Type

Gold coins were regularly issued in six denominations comprising eleven principal types, excluding the early dates. The types are: small (1849–54) and large (1854–89) gold dollars; Liberty (1840–1907) and Indian Head (1908–29) quarter eagles ($2.50); three dollars (1854–89); Liberty (1839–1908) and Indian Head (1908–29) half eagles ($5); Liberty (1840–1907) and Indian Head (1907–33) eagles ($10); and Liberty Head (1850–1907) and Standing Liberty (1907–32) double eagles ($20).

HALF EAGLES:

Bust Type

Coronet Type
without motto

Coronet Type
with motto

The rarest of the regular issue coins is the $3 value. It was introduced in 1854 in conjunction with the reduction of the letter rate to 3¢ and was intended to facilitate postal transactions. The coin was not popular and was discontinued in 1889. During its 35 years of existence, the mintage totaled only about a half-million pieces and many of these were subsequently melted down.

New collectors often ask why the $20 coin, the largest denomination regularly issued, was not called the eagle and the other pieces fractions thereof. The answer is simple; the first gold coins struck

President Theodore Roosevelt objected to the Deity's name on our coins, and some of the $10 and $20 pieces of 1907 and 1908 are without the "In God We Trust." Congress restored it in 1908, for all succeeding issues.

were the $5 and $10 pieces of 1795. The unit designation of "eagle" was given to the larger coin, the $10. The $20 piece was not introduced until 55 years later in 1850 and by that time the $10 eagle

Double Eagle, Coronet Type without motto

was firmly established. The $1 and $3 pieces were also introduced later, in 1849 and 1854 respectively. As they were not convenient fractions in the eagle scheme they have always been referred to as just one-dollar and three-dollar gold pieces.

The high relief, Roman numeral double eagle of 1907 is usually regarded as the most beautiful coin ever produced at the U.S. mint. It was designed by the noted sculptor, August St. Gaudens.

As gold is a comparatively soft metal, easily scratched and dented, gold coins must be handled with extra care. They are safest when encased in lucite holders; these holders are available for sets or single coins.

The $50 "Half-Union" is one of the rarest gold coins in the world; only two pieces were struck. The coins, a full eighth of an inch thick, are both in the Smithsonian Institution at Washington, D.C., but were at one time in private hands. In 1909 they were sold for $10,000 each, a world's record price for a single coin.

Watching for coins and collecting them is one of the most popular pastimes in America today. The hobby has stood the test of time and from all indications it will continue to grow in the years to come. Every collector has spent many pleasant hours arranging and studying his coins, and at the same time acquiring experience, knowledge and insight into some of the world's history.

II. GLOSSARY OF COIN FACTS

Altered Dates: Dates of common coins are sometimes unscrupulously altered to make them appear as other (and rarer) coins. By way of example, 1944 D cents are often encountered with the first "4" altered to a "1" so as to appear as 1914 D's. These altered dates can be recognized, however, by the "VDB" on the truncation of the bust, which does not appear on the genuine 1914 D cents.

Art on American Coins: For the most part, the early coinage of the United States places no great stress on artistic merit. The ban on personal portraits led to the use of Liberty heads in a diversity of forms and with rather poor execution. The exquisite flying eagle reverse of the Gobrecht dollars was a pleasant exception to a depressing general rule. Later in the century, the Barber and Morgan Liberty Head types represented another great advance, as did their predecessor, the Liberty Seated type.

The same claim may be made equally convincingly for the magnificent eagles and double eagles designed by Augustus Saint-Gaudens after the turn of the twentieth century. The handsome Indian Head incuse types of Bela Pratt, issued about the same time, are not unworthy of being ranked in the same illustrious company.

The appearance of the beautiful Lincoln Head cent in 1909 broke with the tradition of never picturing an actual person on U.S. coinage. It is significant that all the current coin types have similar portraits on the obverse—Thomas Jefferson on the nickel; Franklin D. Roosevelt on the dime; George Washington on the quarter; and Benjamin Franklin on the half dollar. The day of the symbolical obverse is apparently finished, and when the present portraits are discontinued, they will undoubtedly be succeeded by other portraits.

Assay: An analytical test or trial to ascertain the purity, weight, and consistence of precious metal in coin or bullion.

Barber Head Coins: Any coins or patterns designed by mint engraver Charles E. Barber but used specifically to refer to the Liberty Head dime, quarter and half dollar of the 1892-1916 issue.

Bit: A "bit" cut off from the edge or from the center of a Spanish piece of eight, and countermarked for currency in the West Indies. They were in circulation until the early years of the nineteenth century. A "bit" is equivalent in value to one *real*. It was a common custom to

Left: Piece of Eight.
Right: 2 bits and 4 bits.

divide an 8-*reales* piece into quarters—hence our expression "two bits" to denote a quarter dollar.

Broken Bank Note: Many of the State Banks which came into existence in the United States before the passage of the National Banking Act

This is not a phony but an obsolete $3 bank note of Adrian, Michigan. Prior to 1861, banks issued their own currency, and the $3 note was a fairly common denomination.

of 1863 became insolvent—they went "broke" and their notes became worthless. Such a note is termed a "Broken Bank Note."

Broken Die: In the early days of American coinage, it frequently happened that the dies from which coins were struck broke because of improper hardening or flaws in the dies. On coins struck from such dies we find evidence in the form of raised lines of metal corresponding to the cracks in the die or extra lumps of metal where a whole chip had fallen out of the die.

Bronze: An alloy of copper and tin, etc., usually consisting of 80–95 per cent copper. It is the world's earliest artificial alloy, and, in fact, was manufactured in prehistoric days.

Bust: The head, including all or part of the collar bone. Almost invariably shown in profile.

Cent (U.S.): This copper coin, authorized by the Mint Act of 1792, has been issued from 1793 to date. Large cents were struck through 1857, after which a smaller size was adopted with far more satisfactory results.

Large Cents. This denomination has more types, varieties and die breaks than any other American coin issued for a comparable period.

The Chain (or Link) cent got its name from the circular chain of links enclosing the value on the obverse. A bust of Liberty with free-flowing hair and facing right appeared on the obverse.

The reverse design was changed to a wreath (Wreath type). The planchets for these were heavy enough for a thick edge; in some cases lettering appeared on the edge, for example ONE HUNDRED FOR A DOLLAR. On other varieties vines and bars appeared on the edge.

The Wreath type was soon replaced by the Liberty Cap type. The bust of Liberty (facing right) on the new coins is believed to have been derived from originals inspired by the French Revolution. At the beginning of 1796 the weight of the cent was reduced. This resulted in a thinner coin, so that the lettering on the edge was dropped and replaced by a plain edge as on the modern cent.

In 1796 the Draped Bust (Liberty facing right) appeared and continued to be struck through 1807.

The Turban Head type (Liberty facing left) was struck 1808–14. No cents were issued in 1815 because of a copper shortage resulting from the War of 1812. The Coronet type (Liberty facing left) first appeared in 1816 and was struck through 1839. A fire at the mint in

U.S.A., large cent,
Turban Head type.

1816 led to the introduction of more efficient machinery and the adoption of improved methods.

The last type to be used on the large cents, the Braided Hair (Liberty facing left) was struck from 1839 through 1857, the last year of this coinage.

Small Cents. These come in three types, as follows:

The Flying Eagle cent was designed by J. B. Longacre, the engraver at the mint. The beautiful obverse (eagle in flight) was adapted from the reverse of the Gobrecht dollars. On the reverse the value is encircled by a wreath of corn, wheat, cotton and tobacco.

The small cents were struck in an alloy made up of 88 per cent copper and 12 per cent nickel. The rather large proportion of nickel had two consequences. It gave the coins a whitish appearance that was hard to imitate. What was even more forbidding to counterfeiters was the high cost of nickel, which brought the intrinsic cost of the metal in a coin to 4/5 of a cent. The high cost was due to primitive mining methods.

U.S.A., small cents.
Left: Flying Eagle type.
Right: Indian Head type.

The last year of the Flying Eagle design was 1858. Longacre then designed the Indian Head obverse, which was first issued in 1859. According to a legend now largely discredited, Longacre's little daughter was the model for the Indian head.

The Indian Head Cent also had a new reverse, a laurel wreath being substituted for the wreath on the Flying Eagle reverse. Beginning with the 1860 issue the laurel wreath was replaced by an oak wreath and a small shield was added at the top of the reverse.

For a number of reasons nickel soon proved unsatisfactory. There was excessive die breakage on the nickel planchets. With the coming of the Civil War the government was cut off from foreign nickel supplies, so that it became increasingly difficult to maintain the coinage of the cupro-nickel cent. Worse yet, the official cent had to compete with several hundred varieties of privately issued bronze tokens.

The passage of the Act of April 22, 1864 solved these difficulties. The government adopted an alloy similar to that of the tokens—95 parts copper to 5 parts tin and zinc. This bronze composition is still in use, having been suspended for several years during World War II. The new bronze coin—reduced to 48 grains—received the same ready acceptance that had been accorded to the unofficial tokens. The circulation of the bronze cent was facilitated by a provision in the Mint Act of 1864 which stipulated that the coin was to be accepted as legal tender.

Late in 1864 a further change was made in the obverse of the new Indian Head cent. The designer's initial "L" was placed on the bonnet ribbon. 1864 coins with the initial are scarce.

The Lincoln Head cent has been struck from 1909 to date. The 1909 and 1910 issues were issued at Philadelphia and San Francisco. Beginning with the 1911 issue these cents were also struck at the Denver mint. The mint mark appears on the obverse under the date. The Lincoln Head coin was the first cent to carry the motto IN GOD WE TRUST. It appears around the upper curve of the obverse. The motto E PLURIBUS UNUM appears on the reverse.

On the early 1909 and 1909 S cents the initials of the designer, Victor D. Brenner, appeared at the bottom of the reverse. The initials were removed from the subsequent coins of that year, but, as San Francisco had produced a relatively small number of coins, the VDB 1909 S cents became one of the most eagerly sought rarities in American coinage. The designer's initials were restored to the cent in 1918, appearing from then on at the left bottom of the obverse. Knowledge of this helps a collector to detect the altering of the 1944 D date to 1914 D.

In 1943 the wartime shortage of copper necessitated a change in composition to steel with a thin zinc coating. These cents were very unpopular, possibly because people confused them with dimes. In 1944-45 the government salvaged enough copper from discarded shell cases to mint cents with a composition of 70 parts copper to 30 parts zinc. Because of the large proportion of zinc these coins were a bit lighter in color than the familiar cents of previous years, but they were quite satisfactory. In 1946 the mint returned to the prewar composition. Beginning with the 1959 issue the reverse was redesigned, with the Lincoln Memorial replacing the wreath and the description inside it.

Civil War Tokens: During the early years of the Civil War the Indian Head cent had a premium value because of the high price of copper. Thus there was a tendency for the coins to disappear as soon as they came into circulation. To make up for the deficiency in the supply of cents, private organizations issued tokens known as "Copperheads."

One of the most interesting of the Civil War tokens is the close imitation of the contemporary Indian Head cent with the inscription "Not One Cent." It has been estimated that over 20,000,000 tokens were in use during the war.

The tokens were the same size as the government cent, and often used an Indian Head obverse which made the resemblance even more striking. The coins were made of copper alloyed with brass, nickel, copper-nickel, white metal, lead, zinc, tin, German silver or silver.

Our first commemorative coin was the Columbian Exposition half dollar. It shows Christopher Columbus and his ship, the *Santa Maria*.

Commemorative Coins (U.S.): As the name indicates, these coins are issued to mark special occasions and to honor great men and outstanding historic events. American commemorative coins make up the handsomest and most varied series in all our coinage. Almost all buying and

The Isabella quarter is the only commemorative of this denomination. It is also the only U.S. coin displaying the portrait of a foreign monarch.

The Lafayette dollar is our only silver commemorative of this denomination and the first U.S. coin to have a portrait of an American president. The statue on the reverse represents a memorial erected in Paris as a gift of the American people.

selling of these coins are for the uncirculated state; the commemoratives have never been intended for general use. As of 1963 there were 50 silver commemorative types, of which 48 are half dollars. There were also several gold coins, mostly dollars.

(Left) Panama-Pacific commemorative gold dollar. (Center) Louisiana Purchase commemorative gold dollar. (Right) McKinley Memorial gold dollar. Only 13 different gold commemoratives have been issued. All of them are scarce.

Confederate Coinage: On the outbreak of the Civil War in 1861 Confederate forces seized the U.S. mint at New Orleans. More than 2,000,000 1861 O U.S. half dollars were struck from the original dies under Confederate auspices.

In addition, a Confederate die was substituted for the original reverse. So far as is known, only four specimens of this hybrid coin were struck. In later years there were some private restrikes of the new coin.

The Confederate half dollar was struck with the old Seated Liberty obverse, but with a new reverse.

The Confederate regime authorized the preparation of dies for a cent. Apparently only 12 coins of the lower denomination were struck. In this case too there were later restrikes.

Confederate Currency: The Confederate States of America issued notes from 1861 to 1864 in denominations ranging from 50¢ to $1000. These Confederate notes, which at one time were found in

The $10 Confederate Currency note of the 1864 issue shows a bust of R. M. T. Hunter, Confederate Secretary of State and a vignette showing an artillery caisson. The 1864 notes were the last issues of the Confederacy.

Southern attics by the trunkful, have become scarce in recent years although many of the issues in very choice condition can still be purchased for a few dollars.

Copper (L. *Cyprium aes*, brass from the Island of Cyprus): An important metal, hard and reddish in color, used pure or in the form of various alloys (bronze, brass, etc.).

Dime: Authorized by the Acts of April 2, 1792 and October 1794, the issue of this silver coin started in 1796 and has continued to date.

The designs of the dimes are very similar to those on the half dimes for the corresponding years. The bust type (Liberty facing right) was discontinued after 1807, no dimes being issued in 1808.

In 1809 the coinage of dimes was resumed with the Turban Head type (Liberty facing left). The motto E PLURIBUS UNUM appears in a ribbon over the eagle on the reverse. Up to 1829 these coins had no indication of value.

With the introduction of the Liberty Seated type in 1837, the slight reduction in weight and fineness was indicated in the same manner as on the half dimes—through changes in the drapery of the seated figure, and the addition of stars to the obverse. From 1838 through 1860, there are quite a few dates with the "O" mint mark from New Orleans. The first San Francisco coins were struck in 1856 and continued thereafter. From 1871 through 1878 dimes were struck at Carson City, Nevada ("CC" mint mark). The 1871–74 Carson City dimes were issued in fairly small quantities and are all valuable. The mint marks for the Liberty Seated type are located on the reverse, under the wreath or within it.

As in the case of the half dimes, arrows were placed on each side of the date on the 1853–55 dimes to indicate a slight reduction. In 1859, again as in the case of the half dime, the obverse of 1859 and the reverse of 1860 are used, so that the legend UNITED STATES OF AMERICA does not appear on the coin. On the 1860 dimes and thereafter, the legend replaces the stars on the obverse.

On the 1873 and 1874 dimes arrows at the date indicate another change—this time a slight increase in weight. In 1891 the New Orleans mint resumed coinage operations, so that the "O" mint mark reappears on succeeding issues of the dime.

The Liberty Head dimes (1892–1916) were designed by Charles E. Barber, Chief Engraver. His initial ("B") appears at the truncation of the neck.

The design of the Winged Head Liberty dime is popularly known as the "Mercury" head.

On the succeeding type, the Roosevelt dime, these inscriptions appear in the same relative positions. The obverse carries the bust of President Franklin Delano Roosevelt; on the reverse the torch of liberty is placed between sprigs of laurel and oak.

Dollar Sign: There are various theories as to the origin of the sign $ signifying American and other dollars. The most reasonable explanation is that it is a variant of the ancient Spanish contraction for peso or piece of eight, which consisted of the figure eight between two sloping lines, thus: /8/.

Dollar, U.S. Gold: The introduction of the gold dollar, authorized by the Act of March 3, 1849, was a consequence of the discovery of gold in California. The coinage of the gold dollar extended from 1849 through 1889.

Dollars were the lowest denomination gold coin issued by the U. S. government. These three different types were used between 1849 and 1889.

Aside from the Philadelphia coinage, some coins were struck at San Francisco, Charlotte (North Carolina) and Dahlonega (Georgia). The branch coinage was consistently smaller than at Philadelphia, and the mint-marked dollars are with few exceptions the most valuable. The mint marks appear below the wreath on the reverse.

Type I is the smallest coin of the series. It is variously known as the small-size type, Liberty Head type, Coronet Head type. It has two types of reverses—the open wreath and closed wreath.

In 1854 the dollar was redesigned with a larger diameter and thinned out to keep the weight unchanged. Liberty received a feathered crown, so this second type is known as the Feathered Headdress or large-size type.

In 1856 the head was slightly enlarged, giving rise to Type III. This design continued until the end of the coinage in 1889. The most valuable dollar of this group is the 1861 D coin, which was struck under Confederate auspices after seizure of the Dahlonega mint.

Dollar, U.S. Silver: This coin, a direct descendant of the Spanish Milled Dollar was authorized by the Act of April 2, 1792 and first issued in 1794.

The early dollars were struck in many varieties and generally in small quantities. They are all valuable, the rarest being the 1804 date which has brought as high as $36,000 in auction sales. The Bust dollars, like the lower silver denominations, featured Liberty (facing right) on the obverse, and an eagle on the reverse. These coins showed no value on the face, but they had lettered edges reading HUNDRED CENTS, ONE DOLLAR OR UNIT.

132

1804 dollar, one of the outstanding U.S. rarities.

The 1804 coin is the great puzzle of the series. Though the mint records claim an issue of 19,570 1804 dollars, the coins with this date are exceedingly rare. On the evidence of certain technical details some authorities believe these 1804 coins were actually struck in 1836 or later. The motto E PLURIBUS UNUM first appears on 1798 dollars, set in a ribbon on the reverse above the eagle.

During 1805–39 no silver dollars were issued, but from 1836 to 1839 Christian Gobrecht, the assistant to the Mint Engraver, executed a series of beautiful pattern dollars which are rare and valuable. For his obverse Gobrecht used the Liberty Seated design which became the

1836 silver dollar pattern designed by Christian Gobrecht. The handsome eagle device later appeared on the regular issue Flying Eagle cents.

standard obverse on the silver coins of the period. For his reverse Gobrecht designed the graceful flying eagle which was later adapted for the reverse of the small cents but which was inexplicably dropped from the reverse of all the Liberty Seated silver coins.

The Liberty Seated dollars were struck from 1840 through 1873. The lettered edge was dropped and replaced by a reeded edge, the value (ONE DOLLAR) being shown at the bottom of the reverse. The flying eagle on the reverse was discarded in favor of an eagle grasping an olive branch and arrows.

133

The first "O" mint mark appeared in 1846, the first "S" mint mark in 1859. The mint mark can be found under the eagle on the reverse. In 1866 the motto IN GOD WE TRUST was added to the reverse, set in a ribbon above the eagle. The first dollar with the "CC" mint mark was issued in 1870. All the "CC" coins are valuable, but the 1870 S dollar is even rarer.

During the years 1874–77 no standard silver dollars were issued, but under the provisions of the Bland-Allison Act of 1878 silver-dollar coinage was resumed with the striking of the Liberty Head dollar.

On the Liberty Head dollars Liberty faces left, whereas on the lesser denominations she faces right. The Liberty Head dollars were discontinued after 1904, but there was one final issue in 1921 under authority of the Pittman Act of 1921.

The Peace dollar issued during the period 1921–35 was struck to commemorate the victorious conclusion of World War I.

The Trade dollars of 1873–85 are in a class by themselves During the Civil War American merchants fell behind in trade with the Orient. To help them compete in the Chinese and Japanese markets, the government issued the Trade Dollar. This was a silver coin which contained 420 grains instead of the standard 412½ found in the regular dollar. The metal weight and fineness are specified on the reverse under the eagle.

The Trade Dollar was the only U.S. coin ever recalled. Although it has slightly more silver in it than the standard dollar, it is not legal tender and thus has no "face value."

The coin is a very handsome one, with a figure of Liberty seated on the obverse—not the same figure found on the standard dollars of the period. The inscription E PLURIBUS UNUM appears in a ribbon over the eagle on the reverse, and the value is stated at the bottom of the reverse as TRADE DOLLAR. The "S" and "CC" mint marks appear on the reverse under the eagle.

Originally the law authorizing this coin established Trade dollars as legal tender in the United States up to $5.00. Subsequently, however, the price of silver declined; Congress therefore removed the legal-tender provision in 1876 and stipulated that future coinage of Trade dollars should be geared to demand in the Far East.

The hope of competing with the Mexican peso was not realized. From 1879 through 1885 only proofs were issued, apparently for collectors. As a matter of fact, there are no official records of any proofs issued in 1884 and 1885, and these coins did not become known to most collectors until 1908. It is believed that 10 proofs were struck in 1884 and 5 in 1885; these rarities are naturally extremely valuable. In the opinion of some authorities these proofs must have been struck illegally by mint employees.

Double Eagle: This $20.00 gold coin was authorized by the Act of March 3, 1849 and was first issued that year, thanks to a heavy influx of gold from California.

There is only one 1849 double eagle known—it is in the official mint collection. The 1861 reverse and 1861 S reverse (both designed by A. C. Paquet) are also notable rarities. On this type the value appears on the reverse as TWENTY D. The mint mark appears on the reverse under the eagle. Beginning with the 1866 issue IN GOD WE TRUST was placed in a ribbon above the eagle.

The double eagle ($20) is the highest denomination regularly issued gold coin. The value was first introduced in 1850, although one coin dated 1849 is in the U.S. Mint collection.

The Liberty Standing double eagle, designed by Augustus Saint-Gaudens, is universally acknowledged as the artistic gem of American coinage. The 1907 coin and some 1908 coins do not carry the motto IN GOD WE TRUST, which, however, appears in subsequent issues.

The 1907 double eagle comes in quite a few varieties. There is just one specimen of the coin in high relief with a flat edge. The high-relief double eagle with Roman numerals was struck on 16 coins. One of these

135

sold in 1956 for $9,250. Another variety has the date in Roman numerals; some of these come with a wire edge, others with a flat edge. There is still another 1907 style with the date in Arabic numerals.

On both obverse and reverse, rays highlight the handsome figures on the designs. Liberty, holding a torch in her right hand and a sprig of leaves in her left, appears on the obverse. On the reverse is a flying eagle even more graceful than Gobrecht's flying eagle reverse. The mint mark is above the date on the reverse.

Eagle: This $10.00 gold coin, authorized by the Act of April 2, 1792, was first issued in 1795 and ended with the 1933 coinage.

The Liberty Cap style (Liberty facing right) had two reverses. The earliest was the small eagle also used on the reverse of the first half eagles. This was replaced by the large heraldic eagle with shield.

Eagle. *Left:* Liberty Cap type. *Right:* Coronet type.

During the period 1805–37 no eagles were issued, apparently because of the steady drain on gold for export. In 1838 the first coins of the Coronet type (Liberty facing left) were issued. Throughout, the value appears on the reverse as TEN D. The mint mark is below the eagle on the reverse.

The Indian Head type, designed by the famous sculptor Augustus Saint-Gaudens and first issued in 1907, is one of the most beautiful examples of American coinage. The 1907 issues have several kinds of edges. On the 1907–11 edges there are 46 stars, while beginning with 1912 the number is increased to 48. The mint mark is to the left of the eagle's claw on the reverse.

Both mottoes (E PLURIBUS UNUM and IN GOD WE TRUST) appear on all the coins from 1908 on. The latter motto is missing from the 1907 and some 1908 coins as President Theodore Roosevelt considered the use of this motto on a coin blasphemous. The following year, however, Congress passed a law restoring the motto to the coin. On the reverse of these coins the value is always spelled out in full: TEN DOLLARS.

Encased Postage Stamps: The shortage of coins during the Civil War led the Federal government to authorize the use of postage stamps as a medium of exchange; that is, as money. Such use of stamps had many disadvantages; they soiled and tore quickly, the adhesive made them hard to handle.

John Gault of Boston hit on an ingenious way to preserve these stamps by designing a brass case that displayed a stamp and yet preserved it from damage. In 1862 he patented his idea. The stamp was placed on a round brass disk, covered with a round, transparent piece of mica and then both parts were fastened together in a brass frame. Merchants and business organizations issued these cases in sizeable quantities, placing slogans and mottoes on the back of the cases to advertise their products.

At one point during the Civil War, U.S. postage stamps encased in brass discs with mica windows were used for small change.

The government issued the following denominations for use as encased postage: 1, 3, 5, 10, 12, 24, 30 and 90 cents. After several months, however, a better solution made its appearance: the fractional currency notes. Soon the further manufacture of the cases came to an end.

Experimental Pieces: These involve a departure from accepted coinage practice. In some cases the innovation is based on a new metal; in others a change of shape may be proposed, as the 1884 nickel with an octagonal hole in the planchet.

Face Value: The denomination of a coin, as contrasted with its *market value* or *premium value.*

Flan (Fr. originally a flat cake or pie): A blank; metal cut to the shape of a coin, but as yet unstamped.

Fractional Currency Notes: A collective term applied to five issues of diminutive United States paper money to relieve the Civil War shortage of coins. All the notes were less than a dollar in value.

Two of the issues actually appeared after the end of the war, the last one occurring as late as 1876. In all, some $40,000,000 worth of these notes was issued. A high amount, in the neighborhood of $2,000,000, was never redeemed at the Treasury.

The first issue (August 1862) carried reproductions of current stamp designs and even had perforated edges; but the notes were ungummed. The size of the notes was approximately 2¾ by 3⅜ inches and they were printed on durable banknote paper. The denominations (5, 10, 25 and 50 cents) were obviously issued with a view to replacing the scarce half dimes, dimes, quarters and half dollars. Portraits of Washington and Jefferson were featured on this issue, the 25-cent note bearing five reproductions of the 5-cent stamp, while the 50-cent stamp had five reproductions of the 10-cent stamp.

The first issue of fractional notes was called "Postage Currency." It had printed reproductions of the current stamps, and perforated edges; 5¢, 10¢, 25¢ and 50¢ values were issued.

The second issue appeared during October 1863 and February 1867. All four denominations (5, 10, 25, 50 cents) carried portraits of Washington. Each reverse had a different color.

The third issue (December 1864 to August 1869) had these denominations: 3, 5, 10, 25, 50 cents (two designs). A great hue and cry went up when it was discovered that the 5-cent note carried a portrait of Spencer M. Clark, Superintendent of the National Currency Bureau. The public outcry became so strong that Congress passed a law forbidding the use of the portrait of any living person on the coins, currency

The lowest denomination of Fractional Currency was the 3¢ note. The government minted a special 3¢ coin to redeem these notes.

and postage of the United States. One reason why the reaction was so strong was that two other officeholders were pictured on notes of the third issue—F. E. Spinner, United States Treasurer, and William P. Fessenden, Secretary of the Treasury.

A 15-cent note intended for the fourth issue used the portraits of Generals Grant and Sheridan. However, it was issued only in essay form, as its regular issue might have started a fresh storm of indignation, despite the fact that these generals were wartime heroes. The providential appearance of the new 5-cent nickel in 1866 helped the 5-cent Clark note on its way to oblivion.

The fourth issue (July 1869 to February 1875) comprised these denominations: 10, 15, 25, 50 cents (three designs).

Fractional Currency, Fourth Issue, portrait of Columbia.

The fifth and last issue (February 1874 to February 1876) was made up of a 10-cent, 25-cent and 50-cent note. Interestingly enough, the top denomination carried a portrait of a Southerner, William H. Crawford, who, however, had died long before the outbreak of the Civil War.

Gold (Numismatic abbreviation AU or AV = L. *aurum*, gold): Gold is an ideal medium for coins of value, being highly ductile and malleable, rustless, and untarnishable by water and acids. Native gold is an alloy of gold and silver (*Electrum*).   Pure gold is too soft for the rough usage to which coins are subject, and therefore is alloyed, usually with copper.

Gold Order: On March 16, 1933 a Presidential Order issued by Franklin Delano Roosevelt discontinued all further U.S. gold coinage. The order also removed gold coins from circulation; made it compulsory to turn over all such coins to the Treasury; prohibited private hoarding of gold; discontinued free domestic gold markets. The order further prohibited banks from paying out gold or gold certificates without permission from the Treasury, so that all gold currency could be kept for reserve purposes.

There are a few exceptions, chiefly for coin collectors and industrial users of gold. The order specifically allows coin collectors and the coin trade to continue buying, selling and exchanging gold coins.

Half Cent: Authorized by the Act of April 2, 1792, this coin had the lowest face value of any issued by the United States. The series was struck from 1793 through 1857.

Alexander Hamilton was one of the initial supporters of the half-cent value. He felt it would aid the poor since there would be many small items priced at ½ cent which would otherwise cost a penny if no such coin existed. But even in those days of low prices there was little demand for the coin; in fact, it was one of the most unpopular ever issued in this country. The coins were not legal tender and in consequence they were often refused in business transactions. This in turn led to great variations in the number of half cents struck annually, many of the coins failing to get into circulation.

At first the Liberty Cap half cents had a lettered edge, but from 1795 on, some coins had plain edges. On the 1793 half cents Liberty faces left; on all the remaining issues of this type, she faces right.

No half cents were struck in 1798–99. In 1800 the Draped Bust type (facing right, and without Liberty Cap), first appeared and continued through 1808.

| Liberty Cap | Draped Bust | Turban Head | Braided Hair |

Half Cent types.

The Turban Head type (with Liberty facing left) is officially listed as having been issued during 1809–35, but actually no half cents were struck in 1812–24. In 1811 all the banks of the country refused to accept half cents, leading the government to discontinue this coinage until the beginning of 1825. Some authorities believe that the spurned half cents were melted down to furnish the alloy content of gold and silver coins of the period.

The last half-cent type was the Braided Hair, 1849–1857.

Because of the unpopularity of the half cents, some individuals and banks tended to accumulate sizeable quantities; and over the years a number of hoards of half cents have been discovered.

Half Dime: Authorized by Congress on April 2, 1792, this silver coin was issued from 1794 through 1805, and from 1829 through 1873.

During 1794–1805 a bust of Liberty (facing right) appeared on the obverse, and the reverse featured an eagle with outspread wings. A ribbon above the eagle carries the motto E PLURIBUS UNUM. A peculiarity of these coins was that the denomination was not indicated.

Die breaks during this period give us the inscription LIKERTY on some 1796 half dimes and LIBEKTY on some 1800 coins.

Half Dime. *Left:* Bust type. *Right:* Liberty Seated type.

In 1829 the coinage of half dimes was resumed, the obverse being changed to a Liberty Head facing left and wearing a turban. The denomination, 5¢, now appears under the eagle on the reverse.

In 1837 the Act of January 18 established a new design and a slight reduction in the weight and silver content. Now Liberty Seated appears on the obverse, and on the reverse the eagle is replaced by the value in a wreath.

The 1837 change in weight and fineness is indicated by changes in the obverse: early issues have no stars and no drapery from the elbow on the obverse, while beginning with 1840 the coins have stars and drapery from the elbow.

The Act of February 21, 1853 authorized another slight reduction in the weight of the half dime. This is indicated on the 1853–55 issues by arrows at each side of the date.

In 1859 and 1860 the inscription UNITED STATES OF AMERICA was shifted from the reverse to the obverse. During this transitional period some coins were issued which did not carry the inscription at all. These half dimes (see *Transitional Pattern*) are the most valuable of the series. Beginning with the regular coinage of 1860 the inscription replaces the stars on the obverse.

From 1838 through 1860 half dimes were issued with the O mint mark. The S mint mark appears on 1864–1873 issues. On half dimes the mint mark appears under the wreath, or within it, on the reverse.

Half Dollar: Authorized by the Act of April 2, 1792, these silver coins were first struck in 1794 and are still being issued.

The value ("50 CENTS") did not appear on the half dollars until the 1836 issue. Instead, there was a lettered edge on these early coins with the inscription FIFTY CENTS or HALF A DOLLAR. On the 1836 and subsequent half dollars the lettering and the motto disappeared and a reeded edge was substituted.

The Bust type (Liberty facing right) was succeeded in 1807 by the Turban Head type (Liberty facing left). The motto E PLURIBUS UNUM appears on the reverse in a ribbon over the eagle. The early half dollars have some curious varieties. Some 1807 half dollars, for example, were struck with a 20 C value (which did not exist at the time) and then overstruck with 50 C. (What appears as 20 C is caused by an error on the part of the die sinker who inverted the 5 and then corrected his error.) One variety of the 1811 coins has a punctuated date (18.11).

Turban Head Half Dollar

The 1806–40 half dollars were struck in fairly large quantities to make up for the silver dollars which were not struck during this period.

The first half dollar struck at the New Orleans mint appeared in 1838 and is extremely valuable. It seems that only 20 pieces were struck. The 1838 O and 1839 O mint marks appear on the obverse. Thereafter, with several exceptions to be noted later on, the half-dollar mint marks always appeared on the reverse.

The Liberty Seated half dollars were struck from 1839 through 1891. Though the eagle was retained on the reverse, the motto continued to be omitted. The value was changed to HALF DOL. Slight changes in the weight of the half dollar in 1839, 1853 and 1873 led to familiar alterations in the design. To indicate the first change, some of the 1839 half dollars were struck with drapery from the elbow on the figure of Liberty. This became a standard feature, although as late as 1845 some coins were struck with no drapery.

The 1853 weight change was indicated by placing arrows on the date on the obverse and rays above the eagle on the reverse on the 1853 half dollars. On the 1854–55 half dollars the arrows were retained, but the rays disappeared. Beginning with the 1856 coins the arrows were dropped.

Unlike the half dimes and dimes, the half dollars underwent no changes in 1859. The pattern of stars on the obverse which appeared on the first issue of Liberty Seated half dollars was retained throughout the "lifetime" of this coin.

On the Liberty Seated half dollars the "O," "S" and "CC" mint marks appear under the eagle on the reverse.

The rarest of the Liberty Seated half dollars is the 1866 date (without motto), only one specimen (a proof) being known. On some of the 1873 and all the 1874 half dollars arrows appeared at the date to call attention to a change in weight. The arrows were dropped beginning with the 1875 issue. Although according to mint records 5000 1873 S half dollars were issued without arrows, not a single one of these coins is known to be in any present collection. The motto IN GOD WE TRUST was placed on the half dollars in a ribbon on the reverse over the eagle, beginning with the 1866 coins.

The Liberty Head (Barber) half dollar was struck from 1892 through 1915. The designer's initial "B" appears at the base of the neck on the obverse.

The designs for the Liberty Walking half dollar (1916–1947) reflect the prewar atmosphere in which they first appeared. The Director described the new half dollar in these words: "The design of the half dollar bears a full-length figure of Liberty, the folds of the stars and stripes flying to the breeze as a background, progressing in full stride toward the dawn of a new day, carrying branches of laurel and oak, symbolic of civil and military glory. The hand of the figure is outstretched in bestowal of the spirit of Liberty. The reverse of the half dollar shows an eagle perched high upon a mountain crag, his wings unfolded, fearless in spirit and conscious of his power. Springing from a rift in the rock is a sapling of mountain pine symbolical of America."

The initials "AW" for A. A. Weinman (the designer) appear on the reverse under the tip of the wing feathers. The "S" and "D" mint marks appear on the obverse in the case of the 1916 coins. They also appear on the obverse of some of the 1917 coins; on other 1917 half dollars the mint mark is found on the reverse, to the left of HALF DOLLAR (the fully spelled-out value). Thereafter the mint mark always appears in the latter position. As usual, IN GOD WE TRUST is found on the obverse, and E PLURIBUS UNUM on the reverse.

No half dollars were issued in 1922, 1924–26 and 1930–32. In uncirculated condition the Liberty Walking half dollar has more rare issues than any other modern coin.

The Franklin-Liberty Bell half dollar, the current type, was first issued in 1948. The initials of the designer, John R. Sinnock, appear under the shoulder.

Half Eagle: This $5.00 gold coin, authorized by the Act of April 2, 1792, was first issued in 1795 and ended with the 1929 coinage.

On the 1795–98 issues of the Liberty Cap type (Liberty facing right) the reverses come in two styles—with a small eagle or a large (heraldic) eagle with shield. Most of the coins are quite valuable, the outstanding rarity being the 1798 half eagle with small eagle on the reverse. None of the coins carries a stated value.

In 1807 the Turban Head (Round Cap) type made its appearance, with Liberty facing left. The value (5D.) was added to the bottom of the reverse, and a ribbon containing the motto E PLURIBUS UNUM was placed above the eagle. On this type the heraldic eagle is used throughout—reduced in size, however, to make room for the new material on the reverse. The 1822 half eagle is the most valuable rarity in U.S. coinage, but there are many other notable rarities in the period 1815–30.

Half Eagle. *Left:* Liberty Cap type.
Right: Turban Head type.

The Ribbon type was introduced in 1834, with a reduction in the size of the coin. The 1838 half eagles struck at Charlotte and Dahlonega have mint marks above the date on the obverse.

The Coronet type was issued from 1839 through 1908. In 1866 the motto IN GOD WE TRUST was artfully set on a ribbon above the eagle without resulting in any appreciable overcrowding. Throughout, the value appears as FIVE D. The mint mark is below the eagle on the reverse.

The Indian Head type (1908–1929) was the last half eagle issued. Like the quarter eagle of the same period, it is an icnuse coin designed by Bela Lyons Pratt and has both mottoes (E PLURIBUS UNUM and IN GOD WE TRUST) on the reverse. The mint mark is below the date on the obverse.

Hard Times Tokens: A series of political tokens issued in the United States during the period 1832–44. As they were of the same size as the large cents they were pressed into service to alleviate the shortage of small change that prevailed at this time, particularly after the Panic of 1837. The tokens must have circulated widely, for the majority of them encountered nowadays are quite worn. Most of the designs allude to

The "Hard Times" tokens issued in the period 1834-1844 were the size of the large cent. Coins were being hoarded because of an economic depression, so various tokens were used in place of true cents.

Andrew Jackson's presidential campaigns and the bitter controversy over the rechartering of the Bank of the United States. Many of these coins are imitations of the then current cent, but with a satirical device and legend on the reverse.

Incuse (L. *incudere*, to strike with a hammer, to forge): When the design is impressed on a coin so that the pattern sinks into the flan, the coin is

The Indian Head $2½ (left) and $5 (right) gold pieces do not have raised edges as do our other coins. The design and lettering are incuse in the planchet; these are the only American coins made in this manner.

said to be *incuse*; if the pattern is raised, instead of being sunk into the coin, the coin is said to be in *relief*.

Ingot (M.E. *ingot*, a mold): Originally signifying a mold, this word is now used to denote any mass of metal turned out from a mold. Ingots vary in size and shape, according to the use they are to be put to.

Intrinsic Value (L. *intrinsecus*, inside, inward): The actual metallic value, as opposed to mere *token* (or face) value.

Lettered Edge: To discourage the *clipping* of coins, some early United States coins bore a legend on their edges. On *half cents* of 1793–1797 there appears TWO HUNDRED FOR A DOLLAR; on *large cents* of 1793–1796, ONE HUNDRED FOR A DOLLAR; on *half dollars* of 1794–1836, FIFTY CENTS OR HALF A DOLLAR; on silver *dollars* of 1794–1804, HUNDRED CENTS, ONE DOLLAR OR UNIT.

Market Value: The price at which a collector can buy a coin.

Milled Edge: A coin rim which has been raised in relation to the surface of the coin. This is done to make the coin more durable and to discourage clipping.

Morgan Head Coins: Any coins or patterns designed by mint engraver George T. Morgan but used specifically to refer to the Liberty Head silver dollar of the 1878–1921 issue.

Nickel (abbrev. of Swiss *kopparnickel*; cf Ger. *kupfernickel*): As a medium of coinage, nickel is usually copper-nickel, or cupro-nickel, namely, an alloy of three parts of copper with one of nickel. Nickel coins were first struck by Switzerland in 1856.

In the United States the five-cent nickel coin has proved highly successful since its introduction in 1866. Abbreviation Ni.

Nickel Five-Cent Piece (U.S.): This coin has been struck from 1866 to date under authorization of the Act of May 16, 1866. The original weight of the coin—5 grams—has always been maintained. With one exception, all issues have had the following composition: 75 parts copper, 25 parts nickel. In the early part of 1942 nickels were struck with the standard composition, but after passage of the Act of March 27, 1942 the composition was changed to: 56 parts copper, 35 parts silver and 9 parts manganese. Beginning with the 1946 coinage the mint returned to the standard composition.

The official appearance of the Shield-type nickels was preceded by the usual patterns. During the first two years of issue, however, a great many additional patterns were tried—busts of Washington, Lincoln and Liberty, and several reverse designs. The original design was kept, with one exception. On the obverse there appears an ornate shield, with the motto IN GOD WE TRUST at the top and the date at the bottom. On the reverse of the 1866 nickels and some of the 1867 nickels a circular pattern of stars encloses a large "5." Rays are interspersed between the stars. Fairly early in 1867 the rays were permanently eliminated.

The first Liberty Head nickels appeared in 1883, which was also the last year of the Shield nickels. The reverse featured a large "V" in a wreath, with UNITED STATES OF AMERICA along the upper curve and the motto E PLURIBUS UNUM along the lower curve. This gave some people

1883   1883-1912

The variety without "CENTS" was issued first, but unscrupulous people goldplated them and passed them off as $5 gold pieces. To remedy the situation, the word "CENTS" was added to the later issues and continued to appear on subsequent dates.

the ingenious idea of gold-plating the coin and passing it off for a five-dollar gold piece. Later that year the motto was moved up and placed just under the upper legend. This made room for the word CENTS along the lower curve.

The most valuable Liberty Heads are coins that were never officially struck by the mint. Congress had passed a law authorizing a new design for the 1913 nickel. But—so the story goes—some employees at the mint struck six Liberty Head nickels with a 1913 date and then disposed of the coins to a dealer. Eventually they found their way into the fabulous collection of Colonel Green, the son of the eccentric Hetty Green who had accumulated a huge fortune in Wall Street. Later the coins were dispersed into various collections. These rarities are valued at over $10,000 apiece.

The Buffalo nickel is also known as the Indian Head nickel. A finely modeled Indian head appears on the obverse. The word LIBERTY is seen at the upper right, with the date and the designer's initial ("F" for James E. Fraser). The 1913 coin has two varieties. In the first the buffalo stands on a mound. In the second the mound has been replaced by a noticeably thinner straight line. The second variety became the standard design for subsequent issues.

The Jefferson nickel first appeared in 1938. A fine portrait of Jefferson appears on the obverse, with IN GOD WE TRUST on the left curve and LIBERTY and the date on the right curve. The reverse features Jefferson's home, and the legend MONTICELLO underneath. The motto E PLURIBUS UNUM appears in the upper curve, with UNITED STATES OF AMERICA on the lower curve, and a curved FIVE CENTS directly above it.

Toward the end of 1942 the quantity of copper in the coin was reduced; nickel was eliminated altogether, owing to wartime shortages, and replaced by silver. To indicate the change in composition, the mint mark was moved to the top of the reverse and a "P" was added for coins struck at Philadelphia. This is the only instance in the history of American coinage in which Philadelphia coins carry a mint mark. In 1946 the original composition and placement of the mint mark were resumed, and the "P" mint mark disappeared.

Numismatics (Gr. *nomismatikos*, relating to a coin, from *nomisma*, a coin): The science and study of coins and medals. Like "mathematics" and similar words dealing with complicated and laborious study, the word "numismatics" is a plural though used as a singular word.

Numismatist (derivation as above): A student of numismatics. Note pronunciation, num*i*smatist. To be distinguished from the mere coin collector, who hoards coins without bothering about their history, classification of types, nomenclature, etc.

Obverse: The "face" or "heads" of a coin; that side of the coin which has the more important device, on modern coins the side showing the face of the sovereign or some other portrait.

Overdate: Until the early years of the twentieth century dates were placed on coins by means of an individual punch for each digit. It was thus possible to repunch a digit should the need arise. In the early days of American coinage it often happened that a particular die was still serviceable at the end of a calendar year. Rather than wastefully discard the still usable die the final digit was punched over, thus changing the date. Examples of this are the 1802/01 half cent, the 1807/06 large cent, etc. In the case of these overdates the original partially shows under the newer one.

Since the early years of the present century working dies have been made from a master hub bearing the total impression of the coin including a complete date. The modern overdate coins—1918/17 nickel, 1942/41 dime, 1918/17 quarter and 1909/08 double eagle—have resulted from a mixing of these hubs: the first blow from the earlier hub, the error detected, and the coin restruck with the hub bearing the proper date.

Paper Money: When the metals necessary for producing coins are in short supply, or the prices of them prohibitive, paper forms a cheap and convenient substitute. The purport of such notes is, of course, a promise to pay, but, unlike checks, bills of exchange, and promissory notes, there is no determined date for repayment. Paper money is said to have been in use in China as early as the ninth century A.D. (T'ang Dynasty).

In the United States, distressing experiences with colonial currency and the Continental paper money during the Revolution made the

Colonial paper money printed by Benjamin Franklin.

Federal government very wary of entering this field. Up to the time of the Civil War the running expenses of the government were quite small and amply covered by land sales and import duties. The issue of paper money was left to state regulation, and the national government did not interfere despite the existence of serious abuses connected with the state-bank issues.

However, the outbreak of the Civil War increased government expenditure to unprecedented heights. Even before the end of 1861 the U.S. Treasury had to take the drastic step of discontinuing the redemption of its Treasury Notes in gold or silver. In August 1861

The first U.S. "Greenback" was the $5 Demand Note of 1861. The figure at the left is the statue of Freedom that still stands atop the Capitol in Washington. Alexander Hamilton is at the right.

Congress issued the first government paper money—the famous "Greenbacks," officially known as Demand Notes. They had no metal reserve and consequently their value fluctuated—sometimes violently—with the fortunes of war.

During the next two years more paper money poured from the government presses—the Legal Tender Notes, which had to be accepted in payment of debts even though they too had no metal reserve behind them.

The National Banking Act of 1863 was a great step forward in many respects. This act chartered "national banks" which bought United States bonds and then left them with the government as a reserve against the issue of their own currency. The government obtained badly needed funds while at the same time the money issued by the banks was backed by the government bonds they had purchased. Subsequent amendments to the Banking Act placed a prohibitive tax on the circulation of state-bank currency, which now permanently disappeared from circulation.

During the later years of the war the government issued Compound Interest Treasury Notes and Interest Bearing Notes which were redeemed after a fixed period. The Confederacy issued large sums of paper money which dwindled rapidly in value. The South never solved its financial problem and at the end of the war had to repudiate its outstanding notes.

After the Civil War the government issued several other types of notes with substantial backing. The Silver Certificates, as the name

The $1 Silver Certificate of 1896 is one of the handsomest notes ever issued. Its theme is "History Instructing Youth." Around the borders are the names of great Americans. Martha and George Washington are shown on the reverse.

indicates, were redeemable in silver. The Treasury Notes were issued to pay for silver bullion and were redeemable in gold or silver up to 1933, when gold redemption was dropped.

In 1913 the Federal Reserve System went into effect, and this led to the issue of Federal Reserve Notes. Currently three types of paper money are still being issued: Legal Tender Notes ($2, $5); Silver Certificates ($1, $5, $10); Federal Reserve Notes ($5, $10, $20, $50, $100, $500).

1863 pattern two-cent piece with head of Washington and motto "God and Our Country." This piece predates the use of the 2¢ denomination by a year and shows the contemplated use of Washington's portrait in 1863. (Actually, it was not used on a regular issue coin until 1932.)

Pattern Coins: Pieces demonstrating a new denomination, a new design or a change in an existing design proposed for adoption as a regular issue.

Premium Value: The price at which one can sell a coin (if above face value).

Proof: A coin with a mirror-like surface struck with polished dies on a polished blank. Usually sold at a premium by the mints. A matte proof is one having a dull frosted surface; in some cases this is specially put on after the coin has been struck.

Issued by the Philadelphia mint in a special, sealed cellophane wrapper, proof sets are made by a special process which gives them a bright, mirror-like surface and great clarity of detail.

Proof sets of American coins, including the cent, nickel, dime, quarter and half dollar for any given year, may be obtained from the Philadelphia mint.

Quarter Dollar: Authorized by the Acts of April 1792 and October 1794, these silver coins were first issued in 1796. Early issues were somewhat sporadic, no quarters being issued in 1797–1803, 1808–14, 1816–17, 1826, 1829–30. From 1831 the coins have been struck regularly to date.

The Bust type features Liberty facing right on the obverse. Most of the reverse is taken up by an eagle—a design that has continued on our quarters to this day. The 1796 coin had no indication of value, but "25c." was added to the bottom of the reverse on the 1804 quarter, and this was continued until early in 1838.

Quarter. *Left:* Turban Head type. *Right:* Liberty Seated type.

The Turban Head type (Liberty facing left) was introduced in 1815. An additional item on the reverse was a ribbon over the eagle, with the motto E PLURIBUS UNUM. There are quite a few restrikes, overstrikes and varieties among the early issues, resulting in a number of rarities. The outstanding one is the original quarter of 1827 with a curled-base 2

151

in the value. In 1831 the size of the quarter was reduced and in order to avoid overcrowding on the reverse, the ribbon and motto were eliminated.

On the introduction of the Liberty Seated type in 1838, the value was changed from "25c." to QUAR. DOL. In 1853 the weight of the quarter was slightly reduced. To indicate this change the 1853 quarter has arrows at the date on the obverse, and rays above the eagle on the reverse. The rays were omitted on subsequent quarters but the arrows remained on the 1854 and 1855 coins and were then eliminated.

The first New Orleans quarters were struck in 1840; at San Francisco the first quarters were minted in 1856. During 1870–78 quarters were also struck at the Carson City mint, and several of them are quite valuable. The mint marks on the Liberty Seated quarters are found on the reverse, under the eagle. Despite the reduced size of the quarter, the ribbon above the eagle on the reverse was restored in 1866 to carry the motto IN GOD WE TRUST.

The slight increase in the weight of the quarter in 1873 was indicated by arrows at the date on the obverse of the 1873–74 issues. In 1875 the arrows were removed.

The Liberty Head type, also known as Barber type from the name of the designer, was first struck in 1892. This was the first quarter to have the full name, QUARTER DOLLAR, spelled out on the coin. The motto IN GOD WE TRUST appears along the upper curve of the obverse, while the other motto, E PLURIBUS UNUM, is set in a ribbon above the eagle on the reverse. The designer's initial "B" is at the base of the neck on the obverse.

Quarter, Liberty Head (Barber) type.

The Standing Liberty type (1916–1930) was first issued only a year before the United States entered World War I. The troubled spirit of the times is reflected in the design on the obverse which shows Liberty holding a shield in the left hand and an olive branch in the right hand. The initial "M" (for the designer, Herman A. MacNeil) appears above and to the right of the date. A graceful eagle in flight dominates the reverse.

On the 1916 quarters the usual 13 stars appear on the reverse. In 1917 the stars were arranged somewhat differently and the eagle was raised a bit. These changes give the reverse a less crowded look.

An impractical feature of the original obverse design was maintained for some time, however. On the coins of the early years, the date was placed somewhat too high to wear well. In 1925 a mound was placed below Liberty and the date was lowered a bit. As a result the dates stood up to wear much better.

The motto IN GOD WE TRUST appears on the obverse, with E PLURIBUS UNUM on the reverse. The "S" and "D" mint marks appear on the obverse, above and to the left of the date. The most valuable coin of this series is the 1918 S overstrike on 1917—one of the most valuable items among comparatively modern coins.

Left: Quarter, Liberty Standing Type. *Right:* Quarter, Washington Type.

The current quarter (Washington type) has been issued since 1932, no coins of this denomination having been issued during 1931. The first appearance of the Washington quarter was timed to coincide with the bicentennial of Washington's birth. The designer's initials ("JF" for John Flanagan) appear at the base of the neck on the obverse. The chief features of the design are a noble head of Washington on the obverse and a standing eagle with outstretched wings on the reverse. As is customary on this denomination, the motto IN GOD WE TRUST appears on the obverse and E PLURIBUS UNUM on the reverse.

Quarter Eagle: This $2.50 gold coin, authorized by the act of April 2, 1792, was issued from 1796 through 1929.

The first U.S. quarter eagles were struck in 1796. The first coins minted were without stars on the obverse although stars were added later that year.

The Liberty Cap type (Liberty facing right) had no stars on the obverse on the early 1796 coins. Later on, stars were added. An eagle above a shield appeared on the reverse. The value is absent from all the coins of this type. All the coins in this series are valuable, the coins being rarer than would seem to be warranted by the mint records of the quantities issued. The explanation seems to be that after 1834 the price of gold bullion increased about 6 per cent. Consequently, holders of gold coins realized a handsome profit by having their gold coins melted down and recoined.

In 1808 the Turban Head type (Liberty facing left) made its appearance. The value ("2½D.") was introduced on the reverse. No quarter eagles were struck during 1809–20. No coins were struck in 1822–23, 1828. The motto E PLURIBUS UNUM appears in a ribbon over the eagle on all the coins of this type. The 1834 issue is the most valuable of the Turban Head quarter eagles.

Quarter Eagle. *Left:* Liberty Cap type. *Right:* Turban Head type.

In 1834 this type was replaced by the Ribbon type (Liberty facing left, with hair bound in ribbon). The reverse is unchanged except for the elimination of the motto. Most dates of this and succeeding issues are considerably lower-priced than the earlier quarter eagles. The "C," "D" and "O" mint marks are found above the date on the obverse.

In 1840 the Coronet type started, with a somewhat smaller head of Liberty facing left. An outstanding rarity in this group is the 1841 proof in prime condition. Another exceedingly valuable coin is the 1854 S quarter eagle. In addition to the Philadelphia coinage, quarter eagles of this type were struck at Charlotte, Dahlonega, New Orleans and San Francisco. The mint mark is under the eagle on the reverse.

Quarter Eagle. *Left:* Ribbon type. *Right:* Coronet type.

Some of the first gold that reached the mint from California was used to strike quarter eagles. They have a special mark (CAL.) above the eagle on the reverse; they are valuable, particularly so the proofs, of which only two are known.   The Coronet type was unusually long lived, lasting through 1907.

Quarter Eagle, Indian Head (Incuse) type.

Coinage of the quarter eagle ended with the Indian Head type (1908–29). This and the same type of half eagle, designed by Bela Lyons Pratt, are the only U.S. incuse coins (that is, with the design sunk into the flan). Both mottoes (E PLURIBUS UNUM and IN GOD WE TRUST) appear on the reverse. The "D" mint mark may be found to the left of the eagle's claw on the reverse.

Recut Dates: These are often encountered in American coinage, particularly on issues of the 1840's and 1850's. These differ from *overdates* in that they are a repunching of the same digit to correct a weak or out-of-place impression. The double outline on such a recut digit or date is clearly visible. Letters can also be recut.

Reeded Edge: A coin edge with lines running across the thickness of the edge from obverse to reverse. The purpose of this is to prevent clipping.

Relief: A design or legend is said to be in relief when it is raised. The opposite of relief is *incuse*.

Restrike: A coin struck from original, official dies at a time later than the date of the coin would indicate. Several U.S. coins, such as the 1856 Flying Eagle cent and several years of the Gobrecht dollar, are believed to have been restruck in the 1860's.

Reverse (L. *reversus*, turned back): The back of a coin, the side popularly known as the "tail"; opposite to the *obverse* or "head" of a coin.

Roll: A standard quantity of identical coins, all of the same type, same date, same mint, and generally in uncirculated *condition*. Purchase of rolls of American coins has increased substantially in recent years, undoubtedly for speculative reasons.

The standard number of coins in a roll according to denomination is as follows:

50 cents
40 nickels
50 dimes
40 quarters
20 half dollars

Rubbings of Coins: To make an effective copy of a coin on paper by rubbing, cover the coin with thin blank paper, slightly moistened; rub over with a finger until the outline of the coin shows through, and finally shade over the design with a lead pencil, lightly rubbed over the whole design.

Series-collecting: Collecting a complete series of a specific design—as for example, the Jefferson nickel from 1938 to date—by seeking to obtain one coin of each date and from each mint and including any significant variety. Several makes of albums are available for this purpose.

Collecting in this manner is most appropriate for current designs or for series that were issued up to fairly recently. When this method is applied to series that were discontinued a long time ago, costs mount steeply. Of the older series, the Indian Head cent is the one most readily within the reach of the average collector.

Small and Large Eagle: Varieties of early American silver and gold coins are described as having a large or small eagle. The small eagle (1794–1798) appears as an eagle standing on a rock, wings displayed, the head turned to the right. The large eagle (1796–1807) is a heraldic type of eagle with a large shield on its breast and 13 arrows grasped in its right claw. This eagle faces left toward an olive branch.

Stars: These have been significant features in the design of many American coins and their number has varied from 1 to 48 stars. Most of the coins issued from about 1799 to the early years of the twentieth century carried 13 stars representing the 13 original colonies.

Curiously enough our first silver coins, issued in 1794, had 15 stars because by that time Vermont and Kentucky had joined the Union. At that time it was apparently the intention of mint officials to add a star for each new state. Following the admission of Tennessee in 1796, for example, some varieties of half dimes, dimes and half dollars were produced with 16 stars.

As more states were admitted to the Union, however, it quickly became apparent that this scheme would not prove practical and the coins from 1798 on were issued with only 13 stars—one for each of the original colonies. Due to an error at the mint, one variety of the 1828 half cent was issued with only 12 stars. There is also a variety of the 1808 large cent with only 12 stars, but this is the result of a die break and is not a true error.

The 1934 Texas commemorative half dollar in honor of the Lone Star state's centennial has one large star on the obverse. The "Stella" patterns have a five-pointed star on the reverse. On the obverse of the Saint-Gaudens double eagle and on the edge of the Indian Head eagle, 46 stars appear from 1907 through 1911. Starting with 1912, after the admission of Arizona and New Mexico, two more stars were added. Perhaps some future coins will have 50 or more stars. Both 5- and 6-pointed stars have been used.

Stella (L. *star*): The $4 pattern gold piece struck at the Philadelphia mint in 1879 and 1880. There were two obverses—a Liberty with flowing hair (designed by Barber) and with coiled hair (designed by Morgan). The reverse in both cases is a five-pointed star.

All the stellas are valuable, but the coiled hair type (10 struck in each year) are much more so. In addition to the stellas struck in gold, others were struck in aluminum, copper and white metal.

Storecards: Large numbers of advertising tokens the size of large cents appeared during the 1840's and 1850's. These "storecard" or merchant tokens advertised many classes of goods and services.

In addition to the political "Hard Times" tokens, there were many advertising pieces passed out by merchants. They are usually referred to as "storecards" or "tradesmen's tokens."

Three-Cent Piece (Nickel): This coin, issued from 1865 through 1889, was struck from a kind of "German silver" attributed to Dr. Lewis Feuchtwanger and made up of nickel, copper and a small proportion of zinc. The coins originated as a replacement for the three-cent silver coins.   The nickel coins, like the twenty-cent piece, had a smooth edge instead of the usual reeded edge. From 1877 on, most of the issues were limited to proofs. The most valuable coin of the series is the 1877 proof.

Nickel-Three Cents.

Only one design was used throughout: a Liberty Head for the obverse and a Roman numeral III, enclosed in a wreath, for the reverse.

Three-Cent Piece (Silver): This coin, the smallest ever issued by the United States, was struck from 1851 through 1873. The initial appearance coincided with the first issue of three-cent stamps in 1851. However, the inconvenience of handling the tiny coins eventually turned the public against them, and from 1863 on, only proofs were struck. It seems that this coin was to be called a "trime" (analogous to the dime), but the new name was never actually used.

Silver-Three Cents.

The design for the 1851–53 issues was a six-pointed star on the obverse and a Roman numeral III on the reverse. In 1854 the silver content of the coin was modified somewhat; to indicate the new composition the border of the star was changed to three lines, while on the obverse the value was enclosed in an olive sprig, with a bundle of three arrows below. Thereafter the reverse remained unchanged, but beginning with the 1859 issue, the three lines of the star on the obverse were replaced by two lines.

The rarest year of regular issue is 1855. Only one issue carries a mint mark—the 1851 O.

Three-Dollar Gold Piece: Authorized by the Act of February 21, 1853, this coin was first issued in 1854. Like the silver three-cent piece, it was intended mainly for buying three-cent stamps. Neither coin received popular acceptance and a change in postal rates brought about the disappearance of these coins.

During the period of issue (1854–89) there was only one type: on the obverse an Indian princess with a feathered crown. This is the same design as on Type II of the gold dollar, also first struck in 1854. The

The $3 gold piece, introduced in 1854, paralleled a reduction of the letter rate to 3¢, and was intended to facilitate postal transactions. Only half a million pieces were issued during its 35 years of use, and all dates are rare today.

word LIBERTY appears on the crown. The reverse features a wreath of tobacco, wheat, corn and cotton. The value and date are inside the wreath. Branch-mint coinage of three-dollar gold terminated in 1870, when the San Francisco mint struck only two of the coins. The mint mark is below the wreath on the reverse. Today only one of these coins is known to be in existence; the second was put in the cornerstone of the old San Francisco mint and could not be found when the building was demolished.

The next rarest coin of the series is the 1875 issue, of which 20 proof coins were struck all told.

Tolerance: All United States coins are alloys with a specified proportion of the amounts of metal that go into the composition of each coin. This proportion is called "fineness." The legally allowable degree of deviation from the stipulated grade of fineness—known as "tolerance"—is as follows:

Silver (dime, quarter dollar, half dollar): 900 parts silver to 100 parts copper; tolerance is a deviation of 6 parts of silver per thousand parts.

158

Cupro-nickel (nickel): 750 parts copper to 250 parts nickel; tolerance is a deviation of 25 parts of nickel per thousand parts.

Bronze (cent): 950 parts copper to 50 parts zinc and tin; no legal definition of tolerance.

Transitional Pattern: A coin issued at the time of a design change incorporating features of both the old and new designs. The best-known transitional pieces are the half dime and dime of 1859 and 1860 combining the old obverse and the new reverse.

Truncation (L. *truncatus*, cut off): The truncation of a bust is the line at the base of the neck, where it appears "cut off." This usually takes the form of a narrow scroll, where often the initials or the name of the designer of the coin appear.

Twenty-Cent Piece: This silver coin was first issued in 1875 pursuant to the Act of March 3, 1875. But it was so close to the familiar quarter in size and design that the public expressed strong dislike for the coins, which were discontinued after 1878. The Liberty Seated is very similar

20-Cent piece.

to the obverse on the quarter; the eagle has a close resemblance to the eagle on the reverse of the Trade Dollar. A peculiarity of the twenty-cent pieces is that they have a smooth edge instead of the usual reeded edge.

Despite the fact that 10,000 1876 CC pieces were struck, this coin is an outstanding rarity.

Two-Cent Piece: United States coin issued from 1864 through 1873, under the authorization of the Act of April 22, 1864. This law provided for a bronze two-cent coin of 95 per cent copper, with tin and zinc making up the remaining 5 per cent. The weight was 90 grains, slightly less than double the weight of the bronze cent authorized in the same legislation.

In the first year of issue, almost 20,000,000 two-cent coins were struck, doubtless in answer to the severe coin shortage that developed during the Civil War. Thereafter the popularity of the coin declined very sharply, only about 3,000,000 being struck in 1866. The annual mint figure continued to dwindle, and in the final year of issue (1873) only proofs were struck.

2-Cent bronze.

Nevertheless this coin is of outstanding interest to collectors, as it was the first to carry the familiar motto, "In God We Trust." It is believed that the Rev. M. R. Watkinson originated the idea, suggesting "God, Liberty, Law" to Secretary of the Treasury Salmon P. Chase in 1861 in the hope that this "would relieve us from the ignominy of heathenism." Secretary Chase liked the idea and authorized designs for a coin to carry a motto for expressing this theme "in the fewest and tersest words." One of the mottoes submitted was, "God, Our Trust," which Chase modified to the form which was actually adopted.

The design for the obverse of the two-cent coin was a shield (very similar to the one subsequently used on the shield nickel), encircled by leaves and topped by a wavy scroll containing the motto.

Type-collecting: Collecting coins on the basis of the design on the obverse. Example: Indian Head cent, Shield nickel. This involves obtaining one coin of each design type. Any date or mint will do. This comparatively inexpensive form of collecting is particularly suitable in the case of the older, sometimes prohibitively costly American coins. Contrast this with *Series-collecting*.

Up-grading: A continuous process of improving a collection and increasing its investment value by replacing inferior specimens with superior examples of the same coins.

Wire Edge: When a coin has a sharp rim around the perimeter it is said to have a wire edge. Some of the 1907 Saint-Gaudens eagles and double eagles have a wire edge.